THE FOLGER LIBRARY SHAKESPEARE

Designed to make Shakespeare's classic plays available to the general reader, each edition contains a reliable text with modernized spelling and punctuation, scene-by-scene plot summaries, and explanatory notes clarifying obscure and obsolete expressions. An interpretive essay and accounts of Shakespeare's life and theater form an instructive preface to each play.

Louis B. Wright, General Editor, was the Director of the Folger Shakespeare Library from 1948 until his retirement in 1968. He is the author of *Middle-Class Culture in Elizabethan England, Religion and Empire, Shakespeare for Everyman,* and many other books and essays on the history and literature of the Tudor and Stuart periods.

Virginia Lamar, Assistant Editor, served as research assistant to the Director and Executive Secretary of the Folger Shakespeare Library from 1946 until her death in 1968. She is the author of *English Dress in the Age of Shakespeare* and *Travel and Roads in England,* and coeditor of William Strachey's *Historie of Travell into Virginia Britania.*

The Folger Shakespeare Library

The Folger Shakespeare Library in Washington, D.C., a research institute founded and endowed by Henry Clay Folger and administered by the Trustees of Amherst College, contains the world's largest collection of Shakespeareana. Although the Folger Library's primary purpose is to encourage advanced research in history and literature, it has continually exhibited a profound concern in stimulating a popular interest in the Elizabethan period.

GENERAL EDITOR

LOUIS B. WRIGHT

Director, Folger Shakespeare Library, 1948–1968

ASSISTANT EDITOR

VIRGINIA A. LaMAR

Executive Secretary, Folger Shakespeare Library, 1946–1968

The Folger Library General Reader's Shakespeare

THE TRAGEDY OF RICHARD THE THIRD

by WILLIAM SHAKESPEARE

WASHINGTON SQUARE PRESS
PUBLISHED BY POCKET BOOKS NEW YORK

A Washington Square Press/Pocket Books Publication
POCKET BOOKS, a Simon & Schuster division of
GULF & WESTERN CORPORATION
1230 Avenue of the Americas, New York, N.Y. 10020

ISBN: 0-671-41018-0

First Pocket Books printing October, 1950

20 19 18 17 16 15

Printed in the U.S.A.

Preface

This edition of *Richard III* is designed to make available a readable text of one of Shakespeare's most popular plays. In the centuries since Shakespeare many changes have occurred in the meanings of words, and some clarification of Shakespeare's vocabulary may be helpful. To provide the reader with necessary notes in the most accessible format, we have placed them on the pages facing the text that they explain. We have tried to make these notes as brief and simple as possible. Preliminary to the text we have also included a brief statement of essential information about Shakespeare and his stage. Readers desiring more detailed information should refer to the books suggested in the references, and if still further information is needed, the bibliographies in those books will provide necessary clues to the literature of the subject.

The early texts of all of Shakespeare's plays provide only inadequate stage directions, and it is conventional for modern editors to add many that clarify the action. Such additions, and additions to entrances, are placed in square brackets.

All illustrations are from material in the Folger Library collections.

L. B. W.
V. A. L.

January 1, 1960

Melodrama with an Arch-Villain

In *The Tragedy of Richard the Third,* one of his earliest plays, Shakespeare achieved a great theatrical success and contrived a play that has held the stage from that day to this. *Richard III* is essentially a melodrama with the spectator's interest centered upon the arch-villainy of Richard, Duke of Gloucester, whose Machiavellian scheming at last gains for him the crown. Richard's wickedness is so complete, and he is so perfect in his role, that the spectator watches with morbid fascination as his misdeeds follow in logical sequence. If Shakespeare had conceived Richard as a tragic hero he would have had to endow him with certain noble qualities to be eclipsed by some tragic flaw, but Shakespeare's Richard has hardly a virtue, unless selfish ambition and desperate courage can be so described. Although the spectator does not identify himself with Richard, as he might with Macbeth or Hamlet, he does give Richard the tribute of his undivided attention because of the very symmetry and perfection of his villainy. Richard may horrify us, but he never bores us.

The date of the play is uncertain, but scholars agree that it follows closely after *Henry VI, Part III,* in which Shakespeare had a hand. This means that *Richard III* probably dates from somewhere be-

From Sir George Buc, *Life and Reigne of Richard the Third* (1647).

tween the end of 1592 and the beginning of 1595; perhaps 1593 is about as close as we can come to its first performance. The events of *Richard III* follow in historical sequence after those described in *Henry VI, Part III*, with a slight overlapping, for Shakespeare telescopes happenings that were years apart and alters facts to suit his theatrical purposes. In *Henry VI, Part III*, Richard, Duke of Gloucester, is portrayed as the scheming and implacable foe of the Lancastrians, the man who slew King Henry and wreaked vengeance upon other enemies in the King's faction. The way is thus paved for his characterization in the play that bears his name.

The influence of Christopher Marlowe has been seen in Shakespeare's handling of the character of Richard III and in the oratorical quality of many of the lines. Marlowe had made popular the arch-villain as protagonist in *The Jew of Malta* and *Tamburlaine*, and Shakespeare could hardly help reflecting some influence of a type of drama then popular on the London stage.

He was also writing at a time when the chronicle play was in fashion. This was a loose-structured type of drama portraying a sequence of historical happenings without much concern for unified action. In *Richard III*, Shakespeare follows the old-fashioned type of historical play in some degree, but he at least succeeds in focusing interest upon one character, Richard. He does not develop the protagonist's character, as, for example, he does in *Macbeth*, for Richard begins a villain and ends a villain without a shade of change; but Shakespeare makes him a living and vivid being, not merely an abstraction of evil. Though he is colossal in his iniquity, Richard nevertheless remains within the range of human credibility, and he has impressed himself upon the memories of more than three and a half centuries of theatregoers as a personality, evil but vivid. The part is admirably conceived to give an actor scope for diversity of impersonation. Richard can be bloodcurdling in his savagery; he can be smooth and plausible, as in his wooing of Anne; and he can summon the appearance of gentle piety, as he does on the platform between the two bishops. On the stage he is never merely a cardboard specter of evil uttering maledictions. He is the very essence of activity and vigor, bustling with life and action. Small wonder that actors have always enjoyed the role.

Some evidences of another type of drama popular in Shakespeare's early years are also discernible in *Richard III*. Thomas Kyd's play *The Spanish Tragedy*, first performed about 1585–87, is a typical example of the Elizabethan revenge tragedy, a play characterized by bloodshed and sensationalism and usually by ghosts returning to see that vengeance befalls their murderers. In the Roman plays of Seneca the Elizabethans found examples of this type of play, which for a time enjoyed an immense popularity. These plays emphasized the artificial cut and thrust of words as well as action, a trick that Shakespeare uses frequently in *Richard III*, especially in the scenes with the keening women. Although old Margaret of Anjou had long since returned to France and was actually dead by 1482, Shakespeare heightens his dramatic effects by bringing her back to serve as a sort of chorus or voice of doom. She is presented as a living person, not a ghost, but Shakespeare finds a place for supernatural visitants with the return of the ghosts of Richard's victims in the night scene before the Battle of Bosworth Field.

HISTORICAL BACKGROUND AND SOURCES*

But not all the theatrical devices in Shakespeare's bag of tricks would have made *Richard III* the popular play that it was had he not dramatized a portion of history of enormous interest to his contemporaries and to the world ever since. Indeed, it is not too much to say that Shakespeare created for succeeding generations a concept of history that has received general acceptance, however wide of the mark it may be in fact. Shakespeare and the chroniclers whom he used as his sources were intent upon glorifying the reigning house, the Tudors, and in *Richard III* the playwright could do no less than make a villain of the king whom the first of the Tudors destroyed in order to gain the throne and establish his dynasty.

*This section is adapted from an article by Louis B. Wright in *The New York Times Magazine* for March 25, 1956, pp. 27, 58.

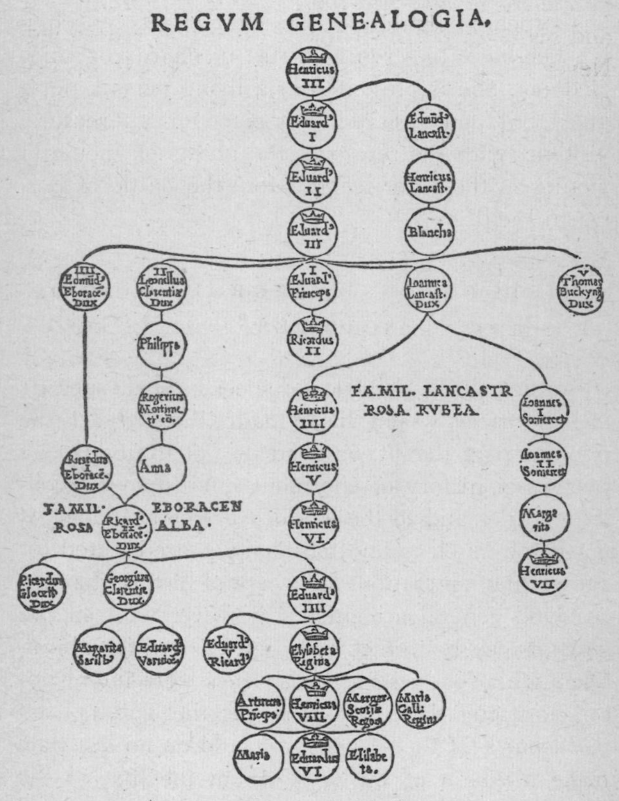

Genealogy of English kings.
From Paolo Giovio, *Descriptio Britanniae, Scotiae, Hyberniae & Orchadam* (1548).

The Tudors, as no other dynasty before them, knew how to enlist history in their behalf. Academic historians are fond of the cynical observation that politicians never learn from history. But Henry VII and his heirs are proof that these cynics are wrong. Never did a politician study the immediate history of the past harder than Henry VII, and he avoided the pitfalls into which Richard fell because he combined knowledge, cunning, and that virtue which Richard never had—patience. Almost immediately after Henry Tudor was given the crown snatched from Richard's battered helmet on August 22, 1485, at Bosworth Field, inspired rumors and stories began to blacken the reputation of Richard III.

These tales got into official accounts of Richard III's reign soon after Henry Tudor seized power. During the reign of his son, Henry VIII, they crystallized into literary art. The first narrative that can be described as powerful from a literary point of view is Sir Thomas More's *History of King Richard the Third,* composed about 1513 and first printed in a garbled version in 1543. More had been brought up in the household of John Morton, Bishop of Ely, whom Richard imprisoned, and his *History* reflects Morton's hatred. Some have even believed that Morton wrote it. Though More's *History* is fragmentary, it is vivid and plausible so far as it goes. It paints Richard as the hunchbacked spirit of evil that he became in the Tudor legend.

The next most important contribution to the official Tudor version was the work of Polydore Vergil, an Italian humanist who first came to England in 1501 to collect Peter's pence for the Pope, then Alexander VI, whose reputation in England as the personification of evil eventually rivaled that of Richard III. Polydore Vergil remained to become an official historian for Henry VII and Henry VIII. Deeply versed in classical lore, Polydore Vergil was a literary artist who made the reign of Richard III the climax of long years of misrule and iniquity. In his history Nemesis at last overtakes the wicked ruler in the person of Richard III, and Henry Tudor, the instrument of Divine Justice, comes to bring order to the troubled kingdom. Later chroniclers, notably Edward Hall and Raphael Holinshed, followed this official line, with here and there embellishments of their own. For his main source, Shakespeare depended on the 1587 edition of Holinshed's *Chronicles,* which he modified to suit his own artistic purposes and the exigencies of his stage.

Shakespeare, more than any other influence, is responsible for the vitality in the modern world of the legend of Richard's villainy. Millions have received all their knowledge of the Wars of the Roses from Shakespeare's history plays, and whatever the facts are, they will continue to cling to the artistic interpretation that Shakespeare wove out of the Tudor legend. The history of the Wars of the Roses has come to be, not what happened, but what people believe happened. And that belief is primarily based on literary art and not on documented facts.

Revisionists have been recently busy trying to

rehabilitate Richard's reputation, but they will have heavy going in the face of the enduring popularity of Shakespeare's version. The zeal to "improve" Richard has led to the organization of a society for this purpose, to advertisements in the London *Times* calling attention to the injury done him, and to books and articles trying to set the record straight.

Revisionists are handicapped not merely by the traditional Shakespearean interpretation, but by the inability of modern readers to understand the social and historical milieu in which Richard of Gloucester and his contemporaries operated. Many words and concepts of the modern world have no application to fifteenth-century Europe. For example, the concept of nationalism and of love of country as we understand it did not exist. The concepts of personal and national "honor" as understood today were foreign to Richard and his contemporaries, though they had formulas derived from feudal chivalry even more rigid than any we know. To comprehend Richard of Gloucester we shall have to divest ourselves of modern notions of political rights and the operation of justice. Starry-eyed political idealists may find it impossible to understand Richard or his conqueror, Henry VII.

Richard grew to manhood in one of the most chaotic periods of English history. When Richard Plantagenet was born on October 2, 1452, at Fotheringhay, in Northamptonshire, where one hundred and thirty-five years later the last Tudor was to execute her rival, Mary Queen of Scots, he came into a world of transition, a world in which all the certainties of feudal tradition, such as they were, had already begun to crumble into doubt, and the ideas of the modern world had not yet been born. The hold of the Church had weakened, and corruptions which within a century would corrode the structure of established Christianity were already eating away at the foundations. All Europe was torn with internecine strife, as kings, princes, dukes, and lesser nobles jockeyed for power and helped each other over the River Styx when it suited their advantage.

In England, the stability that seemed to be promised by the strong rulers, Henry IV and Henry V, of the House of Lancaster, collapsed when Henry V died in 1422 leaving a witless child nine months old to succeed him as Henry VI. The three plays on the reign of Henry VI, which may represent some of Shakespeare's earliest work for the theatre, have given the English-speaking people a familiarity with, if not necessarily an accurate knowledge of, the events of Henry VI's long and troubled reign, culminating in the seizure of the throne in 1461 by Richard of Gloucester's handsome and talented brother, Edward IV. The feuds between the Lancastrians and the Yorkists from the death of Henry V in 1422 to the accession of Henry VII in 1485 bathed England in blood and kept the kingdom in constant turmoil.

We must remember that violence was a way of

life. The crown of England belonged to him who could seize it and keep a head upon his shoulders to wear it. Though there was much talk of royal birth and rightful claims to the throne, the rule of England depended upon naked power and the capacity to execute rival claimants to authority. During the minority of Henry VI, Lancastrians and Yorkists struggled for the upper hand. When Edward, Duke of York, defeated the Lancastrians in March, 1461, and sent Henry VI and his wife fleeing into Scotland, he was not yet turned nineteen. Proclaimed King on March 4, he led his victorious followers to yet another crushing defeat of the Lancastrians at Towton on March 29. The flower of the Lancastrian nobility lay dead, the discredited King—little better than a half-wit mumbling pious platitudes—was a fugitive, and the prospects looked bright for a strong and vigorous rule of the sort that Henry V had given England. Edward's failure to provide such a rule may help to account for the later character and actions of his beloved brother, Richard, Duke of Gloucester.

Edward IV had the physical and mental attributes that ought to have made him a great king. But he had two fatal weaknesses: laziness and the love of luxury. Strong and handsome, he appealed to women and had more than the normal man's lust after feminine charms. Instead of making a marriage with a princess of France or someone else who would have strengthened his position, he affronted the powerful Earl of Warwick, the "Kingmaker," by marrying the widow of one of his enemies, the beautiful Elizabeth Woodville, and by bringing to his court a crowd of ambitious and hungry Woodvilles. These upstarts, as the old nobility called them, made no effort to be tactful. They jostled ancient Yorkists and newly won Lancastrians and made enemies for the King at every turn.

Richard of Gloucester had no love for the Woodvilles. He looked upon them as caterpillars of the commonwealth, devouring the substance of better men. Worse than that, he believed that they curried favor with the King by encouraging his worst vices. To be sure, some of the Woodvilles were brilliant, clever, and learned. For example, Anthony Woodville, Earl Rivers, brother of the Queen, was a humanist, much taken with the new learning that was already sweeping Italy and in the next century would transform the intellectual atmosphere of England. But Richard of Gloucester was a stern man more concerned with the King's duty than with such trifles as Earl Rivers' translation of *The Dictes and Sayings of the Philosophers,* which a man named William Caxton produced in 1477 at Westminster on a new thing called a printing press. Clever and bright though the Woodvilles might be, the whole gang of the Queen's kin, Richard believed, were intent upon inducing the King to waste his time in dalliance while they engrossed his power.

Edward needed little encouragement to fritter away his time and strength. About 1476 he fell under the spell of an enchantress named Jane Shore, wife of William Shore, a London tradesman, who received the King's protection in exchange for his wife's virtue, or what passed for it. Jane was lovely and gay and Edward IV was happy to spend many hours in her arms while Richard fumed bitterly at the neglect of the King's duties.

Though Edward had all the physical qualities that Richard lacked, there is no evidence that the younger brother was envious or jealous of Edward. On the contrary, he showed his love and loyalty throughout his life. He wanted him to be a great king. And his disappointment was intense when Edward let pleasures and idleness come between himself and duty.

Richard at heart was a Puritan before his time. He had had a stern bringing up. Part of his boyhood he spent away from courts in a remote castle on the Yorkshire moors. Sickly and frail, by sheer determination of will he had developed his physical strength and learned the arts of war. His right shoulder and side were better developed than his left, though there is no evidence that he was a hunchback as More and later writers pictured him. He was slightly drawn on one side, but he could bear his arms like a soldier and he learned to swing a mace and handle a sword with the best knights of the day.

During the years of Edward's reign, Richard led his armies in the field, put down insurrections, and harried his enemies. He proved one of the ablest

King Richard III and Queen Anne.
From Horace Walpole, *Historic Doubts on the Life and Reign of King Richard the Third* (1768).

generals the Yorkists had produced, and Edward owed much of his power to his younger brother's military ability. At the battle of Tewkesbury in 1471 his valor and skill were determining factors in that final and disastrous rout of the Lancastrians. Prince Edward, son of Henry VI, died on that field, but there is no evidence that Richard slew him, as Shakespeare and his sources declare. In Yorkshire where, as Warden of the Western Marches, Richard represented the royal authority, he proved an able and conscientious administrator, and the records indicate that he was respected and loved by Yorkshiremen. He and his wife, Anne, became members of the York Guild of Corpus Christi and walked in the annual Corpus Christi procession in that year.

Despite his slight physical deformity, Richard, like his handsome royal brother, was attractive to women. Shakespeare makes him woo and win Anne Neville, widow of the slain Prince Edward, on the way to the funeral of murdered Henry VI. Shakespeare also makes Richard boast to the widow that it was he who had slain Prince Edward, slain him for love of her. The wooing of Anne is pure fiction. She was captured by Richard's brother, the Duke of Clarence, who later sought to prevent Richard's seeing her. Richard and Anne had known each other since they were children. Richard, it should be remembered, had spent several years in the household of Anne's father, the Earl of Warwick, at Middleham in Yorkshire. Richard apparently was genuinely in love with her and won her consent to marriage in the winter of 1472. They returned to Middleham to make their home in a castle they had known before.

Much has been made of the execution of George, Duke of Clarence, brother of King Edward and Richard. Shakespeare makes Richard responsible for his death at the hands of two murderers who drown him in a butt of malmsey. The records show that Clarence was legally executed for treason, and that he richly deserved it. He had betrayed the King on more than one occasion and was utterly irresponsible and unstable. Oddly enough, there are indications that he was drowned, as the legend says, in a barrel of wine. When faced with a choice of methods of execution, the madcap Duke may have elected drowning in malmsey, a sweet death, he would have said. At least that is the conclusion of Richard's latest biographer, Paul Murray Kendall, in his *Richard the Third.*

The greatest blot on Richard's reputation is the murder in the Tower of London of the little princes, his nephews. Edward IV had died of a stroke on April 9, 1483, while Richard of Gloucester was far away in Yorkshire. The Woodvilles, kin of the Queen, had tried at once to seize power and had proclaimed Edward's twelve-year-old son and heir King Edward V. His younger brother was the Duke of York. Richard had been named in his brother's will Lord Protector, but the Woodvilles were determined not to let him serve as Regent. For Richard to become Regent would mean their eclipse at court. In a tug of war over the boy-king, Richard gained control and placed Edward and his brother in the Tower for safekeeping.

In the meantime, Henry Stafford, Duke of Buckingham, offered Richard his aid. Already a powerful man, Buckingham saw his opportunity to rise still further and to supplant the Queen's hated family. Buckingham's influence appears to have been paramount in deciding Richard to seize the crown for himself after first declaring his brother's sons bastards. Not long afterward the little princes no longer were seen in the Tower yard and rumors blew about that they had met their deaths at the hands of murderers. Who instigated the murders? It may have been Richard. He had reason to want them dead. They were more Woodville than children of his brother, that was certain, but he was shrewd enough to realize that their murder would be too unpopular to risk. The murders may have been inspired by "high-reaching Buckingham." In a popular reaction against the King for the murder of the princes, Richard would have to depend more and more upon Buckingham. Buckingham was reaching for power, and he would have stopped at nothing to place Richard under his influence. The fact is that nobody can prove how the little princes died. Long afterward the chroniclers trumped up a "confession" by Sir James Tyrrel that gives the familiar story of their being smothered in their bedclothes and buried under a stair in the Tower.

In his brief reign Richard III laid the foundation

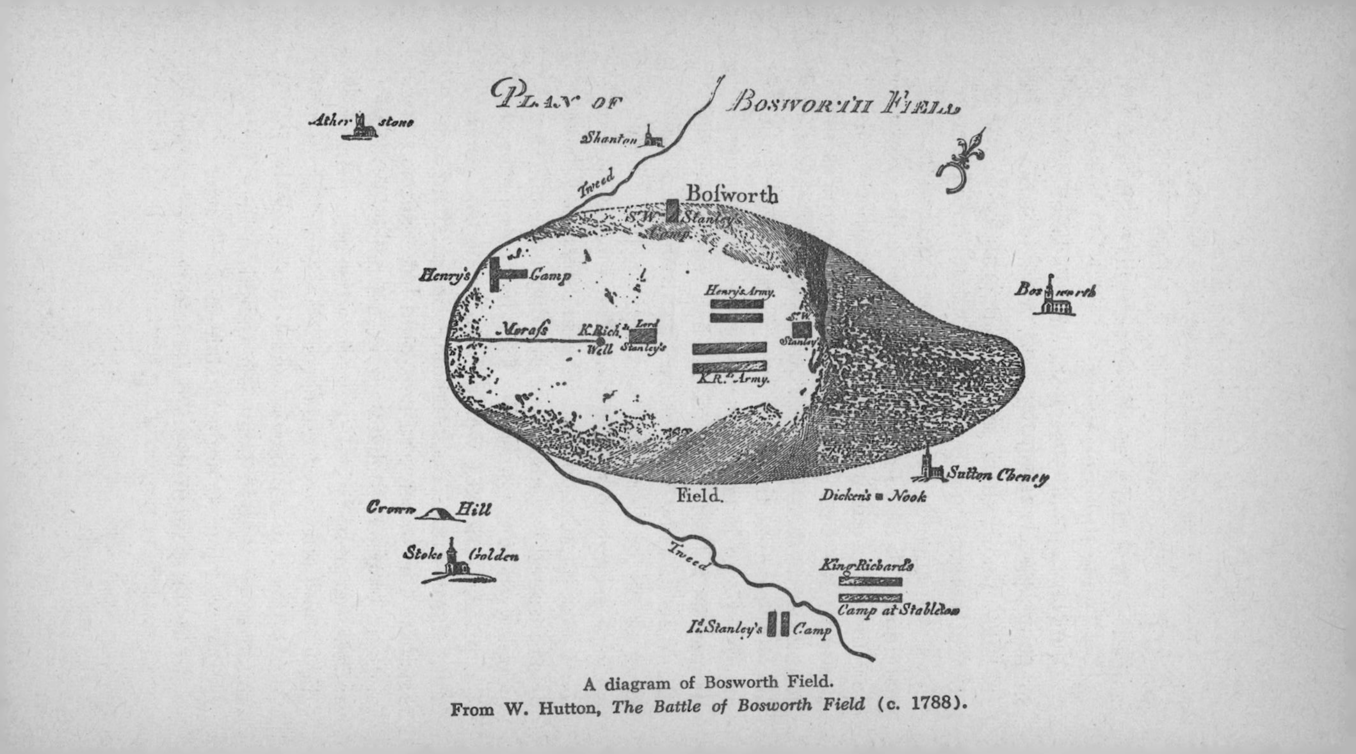

A diagram of Bosworth Field.
From W. Hutton, *The Battle of Bosworth Field* (c. 1788).

for some innovations designed to give the kingdom better government. He established the Council of the North and increased the importance of the great council at Westminster. Both the Council of the North and the Privy Council became important instruments of government in the hands of the Tudors. Richard also set about encouraging trade and cultivating the rising merchant class. But misfortune dogged him. His own son and heir died and Anne, the mother, soon followed. He became gloomy and moody. And news reached him that Henry Tudor was planning an invasion from France.

Henry Tudor at length arrived at Milford Haven on the Welsh coast on August 7, 1485. Claiming descent from Cadwallader, mythical King of Wales, Henry invoked the spirit of the Bards and promised the Welsh lands and spoil to join his forces. Gradually he gained followers and marched toward the Midlands, where he hoped to recruit his strength before making a bid for London. Not far from Leicester, on the barren field of Bosworth, Henry Tudor at last met Richard III. On Sunday, August 21, their forces stood watching each other. Lord Stanley was nearby, with something like 4,000 men, and nobody knew which side he would take. The total number of men involved was probably less than 20,000 on all sides. Stanley was waiting to throw in his men on the winning side, and he did not yet know which that would be. This sort of behavior was perfectly understood by both Richard and Henry, though it may seem to us something less than cricket. At length on Monday, August 22, the battle was joined. As Richard with a small group charged straight for Henry Tudor's standard, Stanley and his men swept down upon his rear. Surrounded and unhorsed, Richard III died swinging his mace. If he cried "A horse, a horse, my kingdom for a horse," the documents do not record it. A horse would have done him no good. He was doomed and he died as he had lived, fighting ruggedly for what he wanted.

Richard's character and his actions will continue to be a subject for debate. Certainly he was not as black as he was later painted. Yet all the perfumes of Arabia and the best public relations man on Madison Avenue cannot quite sweeten his reputation. He was able, ruthless, brutal, and ambitious. Like every other sovereign of his time, including his conqueror, he was ready to gain and hold his crown by the speedy execution of his enemies. Richard III failed. Henry VII succeeded. That made the difference.

Henry Tudor had reason to want to blacken Richard's name and damage the claims of all rivals to the throne: his own claim was none too strong. He was the son of Edmund Tudor and Margaret Beaufort, both of whom were of royal blood, though their royalty was somewhat tainted by the bar sinister. Henry was the grandson of Owen Tudor, a Welsh adventurer who sang his way into the favor of "fair Kate," widow of Henry V. Katherine bore him three sons, of whom Henry's father was the second, but unfortunately they were all born without benefit of clergy. On his mother's side, Henry Tudor was the great-great grandson of John of Gaunt (son of Edward III) and Katherine Swynford, his entrancing mistress. Though Richard II long ago had made all this legitimate by royal decree and had given the family the name of Beaufort, Henry Tudor nevertheless felt uneasy in his pretensions and was glad to trace his ancestry back to Cadwallader and even to King Arthur himself. And just to make all safe for his own heirs, he married Elizabeth of York, daughter of King Edward IV. The first Tudor was a careful man.

STAGE HISTORY

Where the first performance of Shakespeare's *Richard III* took place is a matter of conjecture, but it was probably at The Theatre. Certainly the title page of the First Quarto of 1597 describes it as lately acted by the Lord Chamberlain's Men (Shakespeare's company), which at this time was using The Theatre. Contemporary references show that Richard Burbage was the actor who played the title role. The play undoubtedly had a long popularity, for there are many allusions and references to it in the literature of the day. So popular was it that six quarto versions of the play appeared before the printing of the First Folio in 1623. The bloody career of Richard as described in the chronicles was the theme for many other plays, poems, and popular ballads. Indeed, episodes from the Wars of the Roses provided the theatre with numerous plays during the 1590's and later, and nearly every company of actors had its play on Richard III. Though Ben Jonson might scoff at drama on "York and Lancaster's long jars," he too apparently wrote a play on Richard III, for Philip Henslowe lists payment to him for a play of "Richard Crookback." Although Shakespeare's *Richard III* was obviously popular on the stage, records of the time and place of performances in the seventeenth century are almost nonexistent. We do have a record of its revival at Court on the Queen's birthday, November 16, 1633.

During the Restoration period, Shakespeare's *Richard III* was eclipsed by other plays on the subject, the most famous being John Caryll's *The English Princess, or, The Death of Richard III,* which owed little or nothing to Shakespeare. Thomas Betterton played the role of Richard in this play. In 1700, Colley Cibber made an adaptation of Shakespeare's play which persisted in the theatre down to modern times. It is a greatly shortened version which begins with Richard stabbing Henry VI to death on the stage; it also shows the murder of the little princes on stage. Cibber eliminated Clarence except for an allusion to his murder, and left out Margaret, Stanley, and other characters. His version required fewer actors and was more easily staged than Shakespeare's original, which may help to account for its long life in the theatre. Cibber himself played Richard for nearly forty years. Garrick in 1741 used Cibber's version and he played the role of Richard at intervals until 1776. Most of the famous tragedy actors of the eighteenth and nineteenth centuries at some time played Richard, but Cibber's version was the one almost universally used. In 1845, Samuel Phelps tried performing Shakespeare's text, but the play was not particularly successful. When he revived *Richard III* seventeen years later he chose Cibber's version.

Henry Irving in 1877 restored the Shakespearean play to something like its original state and played the role of Richard himself. Other producers of the late nineteenth and twentieth centuries in the main have stuck to Shakespeare's text, but some of Cibber's stage business has become traditional. *Richard III*, like *Hamlet*, requires judicious cutting for presentation on the modern stage. For one thing, it is much too long for an evening's performance.

In America, *Richard III* from the eighteenth century onward was one of the most popular of Shakespeare's plays. The versions acted frequently owed much to Cibber or some other adapter, but whatever the source of the acting texts, the play gained prestige by being advertised as "by William Shakespeare." George Frederick Cook, Junius Brutus Booth, Edwin Booth, and a host of lesser Richards hissed their villainy into the consciousness of Americans in theatres and in improvised playhouses from New York to the most distant frontier outposts.

Richard III was a favorite play on the showboats on the Mississippi and in the repertory companies which played in barns and halls on the frontier long before the railroads got there. In 1767, a performance of *Richard III* was chosen as the means of entertaining a delegation of Cherokee Indian chiefs on a diplomatic mission in New York. A New York paper reported that the Indians regarded *Richard III* "with seriousness and attention," and perhaps with some wonderment at this revelation of the white man's bloodthirsty iniquity.

THE TEXT

The textual problem of *Richard III* is complicated, and no explanation of the variations in the early versions is completely satisfactory. Sir Edmund Chambers' discussion of the relationships between the Quartos and the First Folio remains the clearest and most convincing explanation of the various possibilities. The First Quarto was published in 1597. This was followed by Quarto 2, 1598; Quarto 3, 1602; Quarto 4, 1605; Quarto 5, 1612; and Quarto 6, 1622. Each new quarto seems to have reprinted the one nearest it in date with the exception of Quarto 5 which in part followed Quarto 4 and in part followed Quarto 3. The copy for the Folio of 1623 seems to have been prepared by taking Quarto 6 and altering it in accordance with a manuscript, perhaps the playhouse copy. Scholars have disagreed over which is the nearest to what Shakespeare wrote. Some hold that Quarto 1 is the original text and the Folio text is a later revision. Others hold that the Folio represents the authentic version and that the quartos merely reproduce an acting version first printed in Quarto 1 of 1597. Sir Edmund Chambers, after weighing all the evidence, concludes that "substantially I regard the second theory as sound."

The present editors have used the Folio of 1623 as their basic text, but like other editors they have adopted readings from the quartos where a correction of the Folio text seemed in order, and added a number of lines from Quarto 1 which are not in the Folio and which seem to be desirable or necessary.

THE AUTHOR

As early as 1598 Shakespeare was so well known as a literary and dramatic craftsman that Francis Meres, in his *Palladis Tamia: Wits Treasury*, referred in flattering terms to him as "mellifluous and honey-tongued Shakespeare," famous for his *Venus and Adonis*, his *Lucrece*, and "his sugared sonnets," which were circulating "among his private friends." Meres observes further that "as Plautus and Seneca are accounted the best for comedy and tragedy among the Latins, so Shakespeare among the English is the most excellent in both kinds for the stage," and he mentions a dozen plays that had made a name for Shakespeare. He concludes with the remark "that the Muses would speak with Shakespeare's fine filed phrase if they would speak English."

To those acquainted with the history of the Elizabethan and Jacobean periods, it is incredible that anyone should be so naïve or ignorant as to doubt the reality of Shakespeare as the author of the plays that bear his name. Yet so much nonsense has been written about other "candidates" for the plays that it is well to remind readers that no credible evidence that would stand up in a court of law has ever been adduced to prove either that Shakespeare did not write his plays or that anyone else wrote them. All the theories offered for the authorship of Francis Bacon, the Earl of Derby, the Earl of Oxford, the Earl of Hertford, Christopher Marlowe, and a score of other candidates are mere conjectures spun from the active imaginations of persons who confuse hypothesis and conjecture with evidence.

As Meres' statement of 1598 indicates, Shakespeare was already a popular playwright whose name carried weight at the box office. The obvious reputation of Shakespeare as early as 1598 makes the effort to prove him a myth one of the most absurd in the history of human perversity.

The anti-Shakespeareans talk darkly about a plot of vested interests to maintain the authorship of Shakespeare. Nobody has any vested interest in Shakespeare, but every scholar is interested in the truth and in the quality of evidence advanced by special pleaders who set forth hypotheses in place of facts.

The anti-Shakespeareans base their arguments upon a few simple premises, all of them false. These false premises are that Shakespeare was an unlettered yokel without any schooling, that nothing is known about Shakespeare, and that only a noble lord or the equivalent in background could have written the plays. The facts are that more is known about Shakespeare than about most dramatists of his day, that he had a very good education, acquired in the Stratford Grammar School, that the plays show no evidence of profound book learning, and that the knowledge of kings and courts evident in the plays is no greater than any intelligent young man could have picked up at second hand. Most anti-Shakespeareans are naïve and betray an obvious snobbery. The author of their favorite plays, they imply, must have had a college diploma framed and hung on his study wall like the one in their dentist's office, and obviously so great a writer must have had a title or some equally significant evidence of exalted social background. They forget that genius has a way of cropping up in unexpected places and that none of the great creative writers of the world got his inspiration in a college or university course.

William Shakespeare was the son of John Shakespeare of Stratford-upon-Avon, a substantial citizen of that small but busy market town in the center of the rich agricultural county of Warwick. John

Shakespeare kept a shop, what we would call a general store; he dealt in wool and other produce and gradually acquired property. As a youth, John Shakespeare had learned the trade of glover and leather worker. There is no contemporary evidence that the elder Shakespeare was a butcher, though the anti-Shakespeareans like to talk about the ignorant "butcher's boy of Stratford." Their only evidence is a statement by gossipy John Aubrey, more than a century after William Shakespeare's birth, that young William followed his father's trade, and when he killed a calf, "he would do it in a high style and make a speech." We would like to believe the story true, but Aubrey is not a very credible witness.

John Shakespeare probably continued to operate a farm at Snitterfield that his father had leased. He married Mary Arden, daughter of his father's landlord, a man of some property. The third of their eight children was William, baptized on April 26, 1564, and probably born three days before. At least, it is conventional to celebrate April 23 as his birthday.

The Stratford records give considerable information about John Shakespeare. We know that he held several municipal offices including those of alderman and mayor. In 1580 he was in some sort of legal difficulty and was fined for neglecting a summons of the Court of Queen's Bench requiring him to appear at Westminster and be bound over to keep the peace.

As a citizen and alderman of Stratford, John Shakespeare was entitled to send his son to the grammar school free. Though the records are lost, there can be no reason to doubt that this is where young William received his education. As any student of the period knows, the grammar schools provided the basic education in Latin learning and literature. The Elizabethan grammar school is not to be confused with modern grammar schools. Many cultivated men of the day received all their formal education in the grammar schools. At the universities in this period a student would have received little training that would have inspired him to be a creative writer. At Stratford young Shakespeare would have acquired a familiarity with Latin and some little knowledge of Greek. He would have read Latin authors and become acquainted with the plays of Plautus and Terence. Undoubtedly, in this period of his life he received that stimulation to read and explore for himself the world of ancient and modern history which he later utilized in his plays. The youngster who does not acquire this type of intellectual curiosity *before* college days rarely develops as a result of a college course the kind of mind Shakespeare demonstrated. His learning in books was anything but profound, but he clearly had the probing curiosity that sent him in search of information, and he had a keenness in the observation of nature and of humankind that finds reflection in his poetry.

There is little documentation for Shakespeare's

boyhood. There is little reason why there should be. Nobody knew that he was going to be a dramatist about whom any scrap of information would be prized in the centuries to come. He was merely an active and vigorous youth of Stratford, perhaps assisting his father in his business, and no Boswell bothered to write down facts about him. The most important record that we have is a marriage license issued by the Bishop of Worcester on November 28, 1582, to permit William Shakespeare to marry Anne Hathaway, seven or eight years his senior; furthermore, the Bishop permitted the marriage after reading the banns only once instead of three times, evidence of the desire for haste. The need was explained on May 26, 1583, when the christening of Susanna, daughter of William and Anne Shakespeare, was recorded at Stratford. Two years later, on February 2, 1585, the records show the birth of twins to the Shakespeares, a boy and a girl who were christened Hamnet and Judith.

What William Shakespeare was doing in Stratford during the early years of his married life, or when he went to London, we do not know. It has been conjectured that he tried his hand at schoolteaching, but that is a mere guess. There is a legend that he left Stratford to escape a charge of poaching in the park of Sir Thomas Lucy of Charlecote, but there is no proof of this. There is also a legend that when first he came to London, he earned his living by holding horses outside a playhouse and presently was given employment inside, but there is nothing better than eighteenth-century hearsay for this. How Shakespeare broke into the London theatres as a dramatist and actor we do not know. But lack of information is not surprising, for Elizabethans did not write their autobiographies, and we know even less about the lives of many writers and some men of affairs than we know about Shakespeare. By 1592 he was so well established and popular that he incurred the envy of the dramatist and pamphleteer Robert Greene, who referred to him as an "upstart crow . . . in his own conceit the only Shake-scene in a country." From this time onward, contemporary allusions and references in legal documents enable the scholar to chart Shakespeare's career with greater accuracy than is possible with most other Elizabethan dramatists.

By 1594 Shakespeare was a member of the company of actors known as the Lord Chamberlain's Men. After the accession of James I, in 1603, the company would have the sovereign for their patron and would be known as the King's Men. During the period of its greatest prosperity, this company would have as its principal theatres the Globe and the Blackfriars. Shakespeare was both an actor and a shareholder in the company. Tradition has assigned him such acting roles as Adam in *As You Like It* and the Ghost in *Hamlet,* a modest place on the stage that suggests that he may have had other duties in the management of the company. Such conclusions, however, are based on surmise.

What we do know is that his plays were popular

and that he was highly successful in his vocation. His first play may have been *The Comedy of Errors,* acted perhaps in 1591. Certainly this was one of his earliest plays. The three parts of *Henry VI* were acted sometime between 1590 and 1592. Critics are not in agreement about precisely how much Shakespeare wrote of these three plays. *Richard III* probably dates from 1593. From this time onward, Shakespeare's plays followed on the stage in rapid succession: *Titus Andronicus, The Taming of the Shrew, The Two Gentlemen of Verona, Love's Labour's Lost, Romeo and Juliet, Richard II, A Midsummer Night's Dream, King John, The Merchant of Venice, Henry IV (Parts 1 and 2), Much Ado About Nothing, Henry V, Julius Cæsar, As You Like It, Twelfth Night, Hamlet, The Merry Wives of Windsor, All's Well That Ends Well, Measure for Measure, Othello, King Lear,* and nine others that followed before Shakespeare retired completely, about 1613.

In the course of his career in London, he made enough money to enable him to retire to Stratford with a competence. His purchase on May 4, 1597, of New Place, then the second-largest dwelling in Stratford, a "pretty house of brick and timber," with a handsome garden, indicates his increasing prosperity. There his wife and children lived while he busied himself in the London theatres. The summer before he acquired New Place, his life was darkened by the death of his only son, Hamnet, a child of eleven. In May, 1602, Shakespeare purchased one hundred and seven acres of fertile farmland near Stratford and a few months later bought a cottage and garden across the alley from New Place. About 1611, he seems to have returned permanently to Stratford, for the next year a legal document refers to him as "William Shakespeare of Stratford-upon-Avon . . . gentleman." To achieve the desired appellation of gentleman, William Shakespeare had seen to it that the College of Heralds in 1596 granted his father a coat of arms. In one step he thus became a second-generation gentleman.

Shakespeare's daughter Susanna made a good match in 1607 with Dr. John Hall, a prominent and prosperous Stratford physician. His second daughter, Judith, did not marry until she was thirty-two years old, and then, under somewhat scandalous circumstances, she married Thomas Quiney, a Stratford vintner. On March 25, 1616, Shakespeare made his will, bequeathing his landed property to Susanna, £300 to Judith, certain sums to other relatives, and his second-best bed to his wife, Anne. Much has been made of the second-best bed, but the legacy probably indicates only that Anne liked that particular bed. Shakespeare, following the practice of the time, may have already arranged with Susanna for his wife's care. Finally, on April 23, 1616, the anniversary of his birth, William Shakespeare died, and he was buried on April 25 within the chancel of Trinity Church, as befitted an honored citizen. On August 6, 1623, a few months before the publication of the collected edition of Shakespeare's plays, Anne Shakespeare joined her husband in death.

THE PUBLICATION OF HIS PLAYS

During his lifetime Shakespeare made no effort to publish any of his plays, though eighteen appeared in print in single-play editions known as quartos. Some of these are corrupt versions known as "bad quartos." No quarto, so far as is known, had the author's approval. Plays were not considered "literature" any more than most radio and television scripts today are considered literature. Dramatists sold their plays outright to the theatrical companies and it was usually considered in the company's interest to keep plays from getting into print. To achieve a reputation as a man of letters, Shakespeare wrote his *Sonnets* and his narrative poems, *Venus and Adonis* and *The Rape of Lucrece*, but he probably never dreamed that his plays would establish his reputation as a literary genius. Only Ben Jonson, a man known for his colossal conceit, had the crust to call his plays *Works*, as he did when he published an edition in 1616. But men laughed at Ben Jonson.

After Shakespeare's death, two of his old colleagues in the King's Men, John Heminges and Henry Condell, decided that it would be a good thing to print, in more accurate versions than were then available, the plays already published and eighteen additional plays not previously published in quarto. In 1623 appeared *Mr. William Shakespeares Comedies, Histories, & Tragedies. Published according to the True Originall Copies. London. Printed by Isaac Iaggard and Ed. Blount.* This was the famous First Folio, a work that had the authority of Shakespeare's associates. The only play commonly attributed to Shakespeare that was omitted in the First Folio was *Pericles.* In their preface, "To the great Variety of Readers," Heminges and Condell state that whereas "you were abused with diverse stolen and surreptitious copies, maimed and deformed by the frauds and stealths of injurious impostors that exposed them, even those are now offered to your view cured and perfect of their limbs; and all the rest, absolute in their numbers, as he conceived them." What they used for printer's copy is one of the vexed problems of scholarship, and skilled bibliographers have devoted years of study to the question of the relation of the "copy" for the First Folio to Shakespeare's manuscripts. In some cases it is clear that the editors corrected printed quarto versions of the plays, probably by comparison with playhouse scripts. Whether these scripts were in Shakespeare's autograph is anybody's guess. No manuscript of any play in Shakespeare's handwriting has survived. Indeed, very few play manuscripts from this period by any author are extant. The Tudor and Stuart periods had not yet learned to prize autographs and authors' original manuscripts.

Since the First Folio contains eighteen plays not previously printed, it is the only source for these. For the other eighteen, which had appeared in quarto versions, the First Folio also has the authority of an edition prepared and overseen by Shakespeare's colleagues and professional associates. But since editorial standards in 1623 were far from strict, and Heminges and Condell were actors rather than editors by profession, the texts are sometimes careless. The printing and proofreading of the First Folio also left much to be desired, and some garbled passages have to be corrected and emended. The "good quarto" texts have to be taken into account in preparing a modern edition.

Because of the great popularity of Shakespeare through the centuries, the First Folio has become a prized book, but it is not a very rare one, for it is estimated that 238 copies are extant. The Folger Shakespeare Library in Washington, D.C., has seventy-nine copies of the First Folio, collected by the founder, Henry Clay Folger, who believed that a collation of as many texts as possible would reveal significant facts about the text of Shakespeare's plays. Dr. Charlton Hinman, using an ingenious machine of his own invention for mechanical collating, has made many discoveries that throw light on Shakespeare's text and on printing practices of the day.

The probability is that the First Folio of 1623 had an edition of between 1,000 and 1,250 copies. It is believed that it sold for £1, which made it an expensive book, for £1 in 1623 was equivalent to something between $40 and $50 in modern purchasing power.

During the seventeenth century, Shakespeare was sufficiently popular to warrant three later editions in folio size, the Second Folio of 1632, the Third Folio of 1663–1664, and the Fourth Folio of 1685. The Third Folio added six other plays ascribed to Shakespeare, but these are apocryphal.

THE SHAKESPEAREAN THEATRE

The theatres in which Shakespeare's plays were performed were vastly different from those we know today. The stage was a platform that jutted out into the area now occupied by the first rows of seats on the main floor, what is called the "orchestra" in America and the "pit" in England. This platform had no curtain to come down at the ends of acts and scenes. And although simple stage properties were available, the Elizabethan theatre lacked both the machinery and the elaborate movable scenery of the modern theatre. In the rear of the platform stage was a curtained area that could be used as an inner room, a tomb, or any such scene that might be required. A balcony above this inner room, and perhaps balconies on the sides of the stage, could represent the upper deck of a ship, the entry to Juliet's room, or a prison window. A trap door in the stage provided an entrance for ghosts and devils from the nether regions, and a similar trap in the canopied structure over the stage, known as the "heavens," made it possible to let down angels on a rope. These primitive stage arrangements help to account for many elements in Elizabethan plays. For example, since there was no curtain, the dramatist frequently felt the necessity of writing into his play action to clear the stage at the ends of acts and scenes. The funeral march at the end of *Hamlet* is not there merely for atmosphere; Shakespeare had to get the corpses off the stage. The lack of scenery also freed the dramatist from undue concern about the exact location of his sets, and the physical relation of his various settings to each other did not have to be worked out with the same precision as in the modern theatre.

Before London had buildings designed exclusively for theatrical entertainment, plays were given in inns and taverns. The characteristic inn of the period had an inner courtyard with rooms opening onto balconies overlooking the yard. Players could set up their temporary stages at one end of the yard and audiences could find seats on the balconies out of the weather. The poorer sort could stand or sit on the cobblestones in the yard, which was open to the sky. The first theatres followed this construction, and throughout the Elizabethan period the large public theatres had a yard in front of the stage open to the weather, with two or three tiers of covered balconies extending around the theatre. This physical structure again influenced the writing of plays. Because a dramatist wanted the actors to be heard, he frequently wrote into his play orations that could be delivered with declamatory effect. He also provided spectacle, buffoonery, and broad jests to keep the riotous groundlings in the yard entertained and quiet.

In another respect the Elizabethan theatre differed greatly from ours. It had no actresses. All women's roles were taken by boys, sometimes recruited from the boys' choirs of the London churches. Some of these youths acted their roles with great skill and the Elizabethans did not seem to be aware of any incongruity. The first actresses on the professional English stage appeared after the Restoration of Charles II, in 1660, when exiled Englishmen brought back from France practices of the French stage.

London in the Elizabethan period, as now, was the center of theatrical interest, though wandering actors from time to time traveled through the country performing in inns, halls, and the houses of the nobility. The first professional playhouse, called simply The Theatre, was erected by James Burbage, father of Shakespeare's colleague Richard Burbage, in 1576 on lands of the old Holywell Priory adjacent to Finsbury Fields, a playground and park area just north of the city walls. It had the advantage of being outside the city's jurisdiction and yet was near enough to be easily accessible. Soon after The Theatre was opened, another playhouse called The Curtain was erected in the same neighborhood.

Both of these playhouses had open courtyards and were probably polygonal in shape.

About the time The Curtain opened, Richard Farrant, Master of the Children of the Chapel Royal at Windsor and of St. Paul's, conceived the idea of opening a "private" theatre in the old monastery buildings of the Blackfriars, not far from St. Paul's Cathedral in the heart of the city. This theatre was ostensibly to train the choirboys in plays for presentation at Court, but Farrant managed to present plays to paying audiences and achieved considerable success until aristocratic neighbors complained and had the theatre closed. This first Blackfriars Theatre was significant, however, because it popularized the boy actors in a professional way and it paved the way for a second theatre in the Blackfriars, which Shakespeare's company took over more than thirty years later. By the last years of the sixteenth century, London had at least six professional theatres and still others were erected during the reign of James I.

The Globe Theatre, the playhouse that most people connect with Shakespeare, was erected early in 1599 on the Bankside, the area across the Thames from the city. Its construction had a dramatic beginning, for on the night of December 28, 1598, James Burbage's sons, Cuthbert and Richard, gathered together a crew who tore down the old theatre in Holywell and carted the timbers across the river to a site that they had chosen for a new playhouse. The reason for this clandestine operation was a row with the landowner over the lease to the Holywell property. The site chosen for the Globe was another playground outside of the city's jurisdiction, a region of somewhat unsavory character. Not far away was the Bear Garden, an amphitheatre devoted to the baiting of bears and bulls. This was also the region occupied by many houses of ill fame licensed by the Bishop of Winchester and the source of substantial revenue to him. But it was easily accessible either from London Bridge or by means of the cheap boats operated by the London watermen, and it had the great advantage of being beyond the authority of the Puritanical aldermen of London, who frowned on plays because they lured apprentices from work, filled their heads with improper ideas, and generally exerted a bad influence. The aldermen also complained that the crowds drawn together in the theatre helped to spread the plague.

The Globe was the handsomest theatre up to its time. It was a large building, apparently octagonal in shape and open like its predecessors to the sky in the center, but capable of seating a large audience in its covered balconies. To erect and operate the Globe, the Burbages organized a syndicate composed of the leading members of the dramatic company, of which Shakespeare was a member. Since it was open to the weather and depended on natural light, plays had to be given in the afternoon. This caused no hardship in the long afternoons of an English summer, but in the winter the weather was a great handicap and discouraged all except the hardiest. For that reason, in 1608 Shakespeare's company was glad to take over the lease of the second Blackfriars Theatre, a substantial, roomy hall reconstructed within the framework of the old monastery building. This theatre was protected from the weather and its stage was artificially lighted by chandeliers of candles. This became the winter playhouse for Shakespeare's company and at once proved so popular that the congestion of traffic created an embarrassing problem. Stringent regulations had to be made for the movement of coaches in the vicinity. Shakespeare's company continued to use the Globe during the summer months. In 1613 a squib fired from a cannon during a performance of *Henry VIII* fell on the thatched roof and the Globe burned to the ground. The next year it was rebuilt.

London had other famous theatres. The Rose, just west of the Globe, was built by Philip Henslowe, a semiliterate denizen of the Bankside, who became one of the most important theatrical owners and producers of the Tudor and Stuart periods. What is more important for historians, he kept a detailed account book, which provides much of our information about theatrical history in his time. Another famous theatre on the Bankside was the Swan, which a Dutch priest, Johannes de Witt, visited in 1596. The crude drawing of the stage which he made was copied by his friend Arend van Buchell; it is one of the important pieces of contemporary evidence for theatrical construction. Among the other theatres, the Fortune, north of the city, on Golding Lane, and the Red Bull, even farther away from the city, off St. John's Street, were the most popular. The Red Bull, much frequented by apprentices, favored sensational and sometimes rowdy plays.

The actors who kept all of these theatres going were organized into companies under the protection of some noble patron. Traditionally actors had enjoyed a low reputation. In some of the ordinances they were classed as vagrants; in the phraseology of the time, "rogues, vagabonds, sturdy beggars, and common players" were all listed together as undesirables. To escape penalties often meted out to these characters, organized groups of actors managed to gain the protection of various personages of high degree. In the later years of Elizabeth's reign, a group flourished under the name of the Queen's Men; another group had the protection of the Lord Admiral and were known as the Lord Admiral's Men. Edward Alleyn, son-in-law of Philip Henslowe, was the leading spirit in the Lord Admiral's Men. Besides the adult companies, troupes of boy actors from time to time also enjoyed considerable popularity. Among these were the Children of Paul's and the Children of the Chapel Royal.

The company with which Shakespeare had a long association had for its first patron Henry Carey, Lord Hunsdon, the Lord Chamberlain, and hence they were known as the Lord Chamberlain's Men. After the accession of James I, they became the King's Men. This company was the great rival of the Lord Admiral's Men, managed by Henslowe and Alleyn.

All was not easy for the players in Shakespeare's time, for the aldermen of London were always eager for an excuse to close up the Blackfriars and any other theatres in their jurisdiction. The theatres outside the jurisdiction of London were not immune from interference, for they might be shut up by order of the Privy Council for meddling in politics or for various other offenses, or they might be closed in time of plague lest they spread infection. During plague times, the actors usually went on tour and played the provinces wherever they could find an audience. Particularly frightening were the plagues of 1592–1594 and 1613 when the theatres closed and the players, like many other Londoners, had to take to the country.

Though players had a low social status, they enjoyed great popularity, and one of the favorite forms of entertainment at Court was the performance of plays. To be commanded to perform at Court conferred great prestige upon a company of players, and printers frequently noted that fact when they published plays. Several of Shakespeare's plays were performed before the sovereign, and Shakespeare himself undoubtedly acted in some of these plays.

References for Further Reading

Many readers will want suggestions for further reading about Shakespeare and his times. The literature in this field is enormous but a few references will serve as guides to further study. A simple and useful little book is Gerald Sanders, *A Shakespeare Primer* (New York, 1950). *A Companion to Shakespeare Studies,* edited by Harley Granville-Barker and G. B. Harrison (Cambridge, Eng., 1934) is a valuable guide. More detailed but still not too voluminous to be confusing is Hazelton Spencer, *The Art and Life of William Shakespeare* (New York, 1940) which, like Sanders' handbook, contains a brief annotated list of useful books on various aspects of the subject. The most detailed and scholarly work providing complete factual information about Shakespeare is Sir Edmund Chambers, *William Shakespeare: A Study of Facts and Problems* (2 vols., Oxford, 1930). For detailed, factual information about the Elizabethan and seventeenth-century stages, the definitive reference works are Sir Edmund Chambers, *The Elizabethan Stage* (4 vols., Oxford, 1923) and Gerald E. Bentley, *The Jacobean and Caroline Stage* (5 vols., Oxford, 1941–1956). Alfred Harbage, *Shakespeare's Audience* (New York, 1941) throws light on the nature and tastes of the customers for whom Elizabethan dramatists wrote.

Although specialists disagree about details of stage construction, the reader will find essential information in John C. Adams, *The Globe Playhouse: Its Design and Equipment* (Barnes & Noble, 1961). A model of the Globe playhouse by Dr. Adams is on permanent exhibition in the Folger Shakespeare Library in Washington, D.C. An excellent description of the architecture of the Globe is Irwin Smith, *Shakespeare's Globe Playhouse: A Modern Reconstruction in Text and Scale Drawings Based upon the Reconstruction of the Globe by John Cranford Adams* (New York, 1956). Another recent study of the physical characteristics of the Globe is C. Walter Hodges, *The Globe Restored* (London, 1953). An easily read history of the early theatres is J. Q. Adams, *Shakespearean Playhouses: A History of English Theatres from the Beginnings to the Restoration* (Boston, 1917).

The following titles on theatrical history will provide information about Shakespeare's plays in later periods: Alfred Harbage, *Theatre for Shakespeare* (Toronto, 1955); Esther Cloudman Dunn, *Shakespeare in America* (New York, 1939); George C. D. Odell, *Shakespeare from Betterton to Irving* (2 vols., London, 1921); Arthur Colby Sprague, *Shakespeare and the Actors: The Stage Business in His Plays (1660–1905)* (Cambridge, Mass., 1944) and *Shakespearian Players and Performances* (Cambridge, Mass., 1953); Leslie Hotson, *The Commonwealth and Restoration Stage* (Cambridge, Mass., 1928); Alwin Thaler, *Shakspere to Sheridan: A Book About the Theatre of Yesterday and To-day* (Cambridge, Mass., 1922); Ernest Bradlee Watson, *Sheridan to*

Robertson: A Study of the 19th-Century London Stage (Cambridge, Mass., 1926). Enid Welsford, *The Court Masque* (Cambridge, Mass., 1927) is an excellent study of the characteristics of this form of entertainment.

Harley Granville-Barker, *Prefaces to Shakespeare* (5 vols., London, 1927-1948) provides stimulating critical discussion of the plays. An older classic of criticism is Andrew C. Bradley, *Shakespearean Tragedy: Lectures on Hamlet, Othello, King Lear, Macbeth* (London, 1904), which is now available in an inexpensive reprint (New York, 1955). Thomas M. Parrott, *Shakespearean Comedy* (New York, 1949) is scholarly and readable. Shakespeare's dramatizations of English history are examined in E. M. W. Tillyard, *Shakespeare's History Plays* (London, 1948), and Lily Bess Campbell, *Shakespeare's "Histories," Mirrors of Elizabethan Policy* (San Marino, Calif., 1947) contains a more technical discussion of the same subject.

The most recent and most judicious appraisal of the place of Richard III in history is Paul Murray Kendall, *Richard the Third* (New York, 1956). Also useful for background is the same author's *Warwick the Kingmaker* (New York, 1957).

The enduring popularity of *Richard III* and related plays is discussed in Alice Perry Wood, *The Stage History of Shakespeare's King Richard the Third* (New York, 1909). Useful information about the history plays will be found in Irving Ribner,

The English History Play in the Age of Shakespeare (Princeton, N.J., 1957).

The question of the authenticity of Shakespeare's plays arouses perennial attention. A book that demolishes the notion of hidden cryptograms in the plays is William F. Friedman and Elizebeth S. Friedman, *The Shakespearean Ciphers Examined* (New York, 1957). A succinct account of the various absurdities advanced to suggest the authorship of a multitude of candidates other than Shakespeare will be found in R. C. Churchill, *Shakespeare and His Betters* (Bloomington, Ind., 1959) and Frank W. Wadsworth, *The Poacher from Stratford: A Partial Account of the Controversy over the Authorship of Shakespeare's Plays* (Berkeley, Calif., 1958). An essay on the curious notions in the writings of the anti-Shakespeareans is that by Louis B. Wright, "The Anti-Shakespeare Industry and the Growth of Cults," *The Virginia Quarterly Review*, XXXV (1959), 289–303.

Interesting pictures as well as new information about Shakespeare will be found in F. E. Halliday, *Shakespeare, a Pictorial Biography* (London, 1956). Allardyce Nicoll, *The Elizabethans* (Cambridge, Eng., 1957) contains a variety of illustrations.

A brief, clear, and accurate account of Tudor history is S. T. Bindoff, *The Tudors,* in the Penguin series. A readable general history is G. M. Trevelyan, *The History of England,* first published in 1926 and available in many editions. G. M. Trevelyan, *English Social History,* first published in 1942 and also available in many editions, provides fascinating information about England in all periods. Sir John Neale, *Queen Elizabeth* (London, 1934) is the best study of the great Queen. Various aspects of life in the Elizabethan period are treated in Louis B. Wright, *Middle-Class Culture in Elizabethan England* (Chapel Hill, N.C., 1935; reprinted by Cornell University Press, 1958). *Shakespeare's England: An Account of the Life and Manners of His Age*, edited by Sidney Lee and C. T. Onions (2 vols., Oxford, 1916), provides a large amount of information on many aspects of life in the Elizabethan period. Additional information will be found in Muriel St. C. Byrne, *Elizabethan Life in Town and Country* (Barnes & Noble, 1961).

The Folger Shakespeare Library is currently publishing a series of illustrated pamphlets on various aspects of English life in the sixteenth and seventeenth centuries. The following titles are available: Dorothy E. Mason, *Music in Elizabethan England;* Craig R. Thompson, *The English Church in the Sixteenth Century;* Louis B. Wright, *Shakespeare's Theatre and the Dramatic Tradition;* Giles E. Dawson, *The Life of William Shakespeare;* Virginia A. LaMar, *English Dress in the Age of Shakespeare;* Craig R. Thompson, *The Bible in English, 1525–1611;* Craig R. Thompson, *Schools in Tudor England;* Craig R. Thompson, *Universities in Tudor England;* Lilly C. Stone, *English Sports and Recreations;* Conyers Read, *The Government of England under Elizabeth.*

[*Dramatis Personae.*

King Edward the Fourth.

Edward, Prince of Wales, afterwards *Edward V,* *Richard, Duke of York,*	sons to *King Edward.*
George, Duke of Clarence, *Richard, Duke of Gloucester,* afterwards *Richard III,*	brothers to *King Edward.*

Edward Plantagenet, son to *Clarence.*
Henry, Earl of Richmond, afterwards *Henry VII.*
Cardinal Bourchier, Archbishop of Canterbury.
Thomas Rotherham, Archbishop of York.
John Morton, Bishop of Ely.
Henry Stafford, Duke of Buckingham.
John Howard, Duke of Norfolk.
Thomas Howard, Earl of Surrey, son to the *Duke of Norfolk.*

Thomas Grey, Marquess of Dorset, *Lord Richard Grey,*	sons to *Queen Elizabeth.*

Anthony Woodville, Earl Rivers, brother to *Queen Elizabeth.*
John de Vere, Earl of Oxford.
William, Lord Hastings.
Thomas, Lord Stanley (also called *Earl of Derby).*
Francis, Lord Lovel.
Sir Thomas Vaughan.
Sir Richard Ratcliffe.
Sir William Catesby.
Sir James Tyrrel.
Sir James Blunt.
Sir Walter Herbert.
Sir Robert Brakenbury, Lieutenant of the Tower.
Keeper in the Tower.
Sir William Brandon.

Christopher Urswick.
Lord Mayor of London.
Sheriff of Wiltshire.
Tressel and Berkeley, gentlemen attending on *Lady Anne.*

Elizabeth, Queen to *Edward IV*.
Margaret, widow of *Henry VI.*
Duchess of York, mother to *Edward IV*, *Gloucester*, and *Clarence.*
Lady Anne Neville, afterwards Queen to *Richard III.*
Lady Margaret Plantagenet, daughter to *Clarence.*

Ghosts of *Richard's* victims.

Lords, Gentlemen, Attendants; a Pursuivant; a Page; a Scrivener; a Priest; Bishops; Citizens; Aldermen; Councillors; Murderers; Messengers; Soldiers; etc.

SCENE: *England.*]

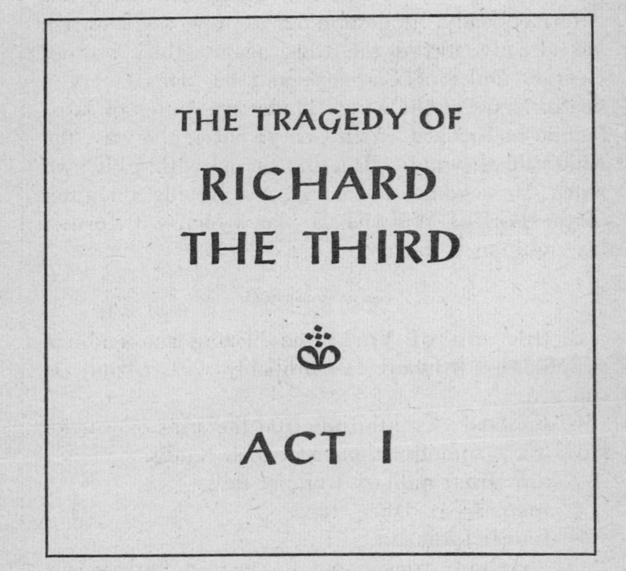

THE TRAGEDY OF

RICHARD THE THIRD

ACT I

I. i. Richard, Duke of Gloucester, describes the triumph of the house of York. The house of Lancaster is defeated and peace has come at last, a peace that makes Richard himself uncomfortable. Believing himself fit only for villainy because of his deformed body, he determines to prove a villain. He has already stirred the King against their brother George, Duke of Clarence, and he plans George's death. News of the King's illness is a source of satisfaction to Richard. With George out of the way, the King's death would place the throne within his own reach. He schemes to marry Anne Neville, daughter of the Earl of Warwick, a plan which will further his ambition to become King.

2. **this sun of York:** the blazing sun emblem adopted by Edward IV, probably with a pun on sun/son.

6. **bruised . . . monuments:** the arms of warrior kings were sometimes hung at their tombs.

7. **alarums:** military trumpet calls.

8. **measures:** dance steps.

9. **front:** forehead.

10. **barbed:** tricked out for war. A barb was a horse's trapping.

16. **want:** lack.

19. **feature:** a handsome appearance; **dissembling Nature:** i.e., nature, which generally disguises the true worth of men by their outward appearances.

22. **unfashionable:** ill-fashioned; badly made.

ACT I

Scene I. [London. A street.]

Enter *Richard, Duke of Gloucester*, solus.

Rich. Now is the winter of our discontent
Made glorious summer by this sun of York;
And all the clouds that lowered upon our house
In the deep bosom of the ocean buried.
Now are our brows bound with victorious wreaths, 5
Our bruised arms hung up for monuments,
Our stern alarums changed to merry meetings,
Our dreadful marches to delightful measures.
Grim-visaged war hath smoothed his wrinkled front,
And now, instead of mounting barbed steeds 10
To fright the souls of fearful adversaries,
He capers nimbly in a lady's chamber
To the lascivious pleasing of a lute.
But I, that am not shaped for sportive tricks
Nor made to court an amorous looking glass; 15
I, that am rudely stamped, and want love's majesty
To strut before a wanton ambling nymph;
I, that am curtailed of this fair proportion,
Cheated of feature by dissembling Nature,
Deformed, unfinished, sent before my time 20
Into this breathing world, scarce half made up,
And that so lamely and unfashionable

24. **weak piping time of peace:** the **weak** pipe is heard in peacetime instead of the shrill fife of war.

27. **descant:** extemporize; ring changes on. **Descant** is a musical term, meaning, as a verb, to improvise a song from a simple tune.

32. **inductions:** first or introductory steps.

34-5. **To set my brother Clarence and the King/ . . . other:** the historical fact is that Clarence had plotted to seize the throne and had been found guilty of treason. Although the King had forgiven some of Clarence's treacherous acts, he finally ordered him committed to the Tower of London and executed. No *agent provocateur* such as Richard describes himself to be was needed to destroy Clarence.

38. **mewed up:** confined.

39. **G:** note that though Clarence's first name was George, **G** could as well stand for Gloucester.

46. **Tend'ring:** showing tender care for; cherishing.

47. **conduct:** escort.

That dogs bark at me as I halt by them—
Why, I, in this weak piping time of peace,
Have no delight to pass away the time, 25
Unless to see my shadow in the sun
And descant on mine own deformity.
And therefore, since I cannot prove a lover
To entertain these fair well-spoken days,
I am determined to prove a villain 30
And hate the idle pleasures of these days.
Plots have I laid, inductions dangerous,
By drunken prophecies, libels, and dreams,
To set my brother Clarence and the King
In deadly hate the one against the other; 35
And if King Edward be as true and just
As I am subtle, false, and treacherous,
This day should Clarence closely be mewed up
About a prophecy which says that G
Of Edward's heirs the murderer shall be. 40
Dive, thoughts, down to my soul: here Clarence
comes!

Enter *Clarence*, guarded, and *Brakenbury*,
[Lieutenant of the Tower].

Brother, good day. What means this armed guard
That waits upon your Grace?
Clar. His Majesty, 45
Tend'ring my person's safety, hath appointed
This conduct to convey me to the Tower.
Rich. Upon what cause?
Clar. Because my name is George.

52. **belike:** probably.

58. **cross-row:** alphabet, which children learned from hornbooks, in which the letters were placed in narrow rows.

61. **for:** because.

63. **toys:** fancies, notions.

68. **My Lady Grey:** Edward IV's wife, born Elizabeth Woodville, was the widow of Sir John Grey when she married the King.

70. **good man of worship:** Richard is sarcastic in describing Anthony Woodville, Earl Rivers, as a man of substance and dignity, since he has no liking for any of the Queen's family.

Rich. Alack, my lord, that fault is none of yours: 50
He should for that commit your godfathers.
O, belike his Majesty hath some intent
That you should be new-christ'ned in the Tower.
But what's the matter, Clarence, may I know?
Clar. Yea, Richard, when I know; but I protest 55
As yet I do not. But, as I can learn,
He hearkens after prophecies and dreams,
And from the cross-row plucks the letter G,
And says a wizard told him that by G
His issue disinherited should be. 60
And, for my name of George begins with G,
It follows in his thought that I am he.
These, as I learn, and suchlike toys as these,
Have moved his Highness to commit me now.
Rich. Why, this it is, when men are ruled by women: 65
'Tis not the King that sends you to the Tower;
My Lady Grey his wife, Clarence, 'tis she
That tempts him to this harsh extremity.
Was it not she, and that good man of worship, 70
Anthony Woodville, her brother there,
That made him send Lord Hastings to the Tower,
From whence this present day he is delivered?
We are not safe, Clarence, we are not safe.
Clar. By heaven, I think there is no man secure 75
But the Queen's kindred, and night-walking heralds
That trudge betwixt the King and Mistress Shore.
Heard you not what an humble suppliant
Lord Hastings was for his delivery?
Rich. Humbly complaining to her deity 80

81. **Lord Chamberlain:** i.e., Hastings.

84. **livery:** uniform of a servant or retainer.

85. **widow:** that is, the Queen.

87. **gossips:** sponsors. **Gossip** is from the Old English *godsibb,* meaning godparent.

89. **straitly given in charge:** strictly charged or ordered.

92. **And:** if it.

97. **Well struck in years:** advanced in age.

99. **passing:** very.

103, 105. **Naught:** Richard plays on the word. **Naught** means wicked, with here specific reference to a sexual relationship.

111. **withal:** at the same time.

Got my Lord Chamberlain his liberty.
I'll tell you what, I think it is our way,
If we will keep in favor with the King,
To be her men and wear her livery.
The jealous o'erworn widow and herself, 85
Since that our brother dubbed them gentlewomen,
Are mighty gossips in our monarchy.

Brak. I beseech your Graces both to pardon me:
His Majesty hath straitly given in charge
That no man shall have private conference, 90
Of what degree soever, with your brother.

Rich. Even so? And please your worship, Brakenbury,
You may partake of anything we say.
We speak no treason, man. We say the King 95
Is wise and virtuous, and his noble Queen
Well struck in years, fair, and not jealous.
We say that Shore's wife hath a pretty foot,
A cherry lip, a bonny eye, a passing pleasing tongue;
And that the Queen's kindred are made gentlefolks. 100
How say you, sir? Can you deny all this?

Brak. With this, my lord, myself have nought to do.

Rich. Naught to do with Mistress Shore? I tell thee, fellow,
He that doth naught with her, excepting one, 105
Were best to do it secretly alone.

Brak. What one, my lord?

Rich. Her husband, knave. Wouldst thou betray me?

Brak. I do beseech your Grace to pardon me, and withal 110

115. **abjects:** lowly servants, with a secondary meaning almost equivalent to "rejects." Richard means that since they are not in the Queen's favor, it would be dangerous for them to do anything she might dislike.

118. **widow:** another reference to Queen Elizabeth's widowed state when she married the King. The King is still alive, although a hint may be intended that Richard would be glad to see him dead.

119. **enfranchise:** free.

124. **lie for you:** that is, lie here in your stead, probably with a pun on the other meaning of **lie.**

126. **perforce:** involuntarily; whether I will or no. "Patience perforce" is a proverbial phrase.

136. **brooked:** endured.

Forbear your conference with the noble Duke.
Clar. We know thy charge, Brakenbury, and will obey.
Rich. We are the Queen's abjects, and must obey. 115
Brother, farewell. I will unto the King;
And whatsoe'er you will employ me in,
Were it to call King Edward's widow sister,
I will perform it to enfranchise you.
Meantime, this deep disgrace in brotherhood 120
Touches me deeper than you can imagine.
Clar. I know it pleaseth neither of us well.
Rich. Well, your imprisonment shall not be long:
I will deliver you, or else lie for you.
Meantime, have patience. 125
Clar. I must perforce. Farewell.
Exit Clarence, [with Brakenbury and Guard].
Rich. Go tread the path that thou shalt ne'er return:
Simple, plain Clarence, I do love thee so
That I will shortly send thy soul to heaven, 130
If heaven will take the present at our hands.
But who comes here? The new-delivered Hastings?

Enter *Lord Hastings.*

Hast. Good time of day unto my gracious lord.
Rich. As much unto my good Lord Chamberlain.
Well are you welcome to this open air. 135
How hath your lordship brooked imprisonment?
Hast. With patience, noble lord, as prisoners must;
But I shall live, my lord, to give them thanks
That were the cause of my imprisonment.

149. **fear him:** i.e., fear for his life.

151. **diet:** physical regime, not merely course of eating.

158. **with post horse:** i.e., as speedily as possible.

165. **Warwick's youngest daughter:** Anne Neville, widow of Prince Edward, son of Henry VI.

166. **I killed her husband and her father: father** is equivalent to father-in-law here. Richard's responsibility for the death of Prince Edward is doubtful. He died at Tewkesbury, perhaps in actual combat. Holinshed, following Hall, is Shakespeare's authority for Richard's part in his death.

Rich. No doubt, no doubt; and so shall Clarence too, 140
For they that were your enemies are his,
And have prevailed as much on him as you.
Hast. More pity that the eagles should be mewed,
Whiles kites and buzzards prey at liberty. 145
Rich. What news abroad?
Hast. No news so bad abroad as this at home:
The King is sickly, weak, and melancholy,
And his physicians fear him mightily.
Rich. Now, by Saint John, that news is bad indeed! 150
O, he hath kept an evil diet long
And overmuch consumed his royal person:
'Tis very grievous to be thought upon.
Where is he? In his bed?
Hast. He is. 155
Rich. Go you before, and I will follow you.
Exit Hastings.
He cannot live, I hope, and must not die
Till George be packed with post horse up to heaven.
I'll in, to urge his hatred more to Clarence,
With lies well steeled with weighty arguments; 160
And, if I fail not in my deep intent,
Clarence hath not another day to live:
Which done, God take King Edward to his mercy,
And leave the world for me to bustle in!
For then I'll marry Warwick's youngest daughter. 165
What though I killed her husband and her father?
The readiest way to make the wench amends
Is to become her husband and her father:
The which will I—not all so much for love

171. **By marrying her which I must reach unto:** i.e., which I must marry her to achieve.

I. ii. Anne Neville is accompanying the corpse of Henry VI to the monastery of Chertsey. She curses Richard for the murders of her husband, Prince Edward, and King Henry. Richard himself enters, and though after a first denial he admits killing both the Prince and the King, he flatters Anne that both deeds were for her sake and finally persuades her to wear his ring and to accept his attentions. Alone, Richard wonders at his success in wooing a woman whose husband and father-in-law he has killed, and ironically comments that he must be more attractive than he had thought.

Ent. **Halberds:** long-handled weapons with pointed heads. Here men carrying the weapons are meant.

3. **obsequiously:** in the manner of a funeral rite.

5. **key-cold:** cold as the metal of a key; a proverbial expression.

As for another secret close intent, 170
By marrying her which I must reach unto.
But yet I run before my horse to market:
Clarence still breathes; Edward still lives and reigns;
When they are gone, then must I count my gains.
Exit.

Scene II. [London. Another street.]

Enter the corse of *Henry the Sixth*, with *Halberds* to guard it [and *Attendants*]; *Lady Anne* being the mourner.

Anne. Set down, set down your honorable load–
If honor may be shrouded in a hearse–
Whilst I awhile obsequiously lament
The untimely fall of virtuous Lancaster.
[*The Bearers set down the hearse.*]
Poor key-cold figure of a holy king, 5
Pale ashes of the house of Lancaster,
Thou bloodless remnant of that royal blood,
Be it lawful that I invocate thy ghost
To hear the lamentations of poor Anne,
Wife to thy Edward, to thy slaught'red son 10
Stabbed by the selfsame hand that made these wounds!
Lo, in these windows that let forth thy life
I pour the helpless balm of my poor eyes.
O cursed be the hand that made these holes! 15
Cursed the heart that had the heart to do it!
Cursed the blood that let this blood from hence!

18. **hap betide:** fortune beset.

22. **abortive:** premature and unfinished.

23. **Prodigious:** monstrous and of evil portent.

26. **unhappiness:** capacity for evil deeds.

30. **Chertsey:** Holinshed relates that the body of Henry VI was conveyed to the monastery or abbey of Chertsey, about fifteen miles from London.

31. **Paul's:** St. Paul's Cathedral.

32. **still, as:** whenever; the word "still" was often used in the sense of always, continually.

42. **Advance:** raise.

44. **spurn upon thee:** trample thee.

More direful hap betide that hated wretch
That makes us wretched by the death of thee
Than I can wish to wolves, to spiders, toads, 20
Or any creeping venomed thing that lives!
If ever he have child, abortive be it,
Prodigious, and untimely brought to light,
Whose ugly and unnatural aspect
May fright the hopeful mother at the view, 25
And that be heir to his unhappiness!
If ever he have wife, let her be made
More miserable by the death of him
Than I am made by my young lord and thee!
Come, now towards Chertsey with your holy load, 30
Taken from Paul's to be interred there.
[*The Bearers take up the hearse.*]
And still, as you are weary of this weight,
Rest you, whiles I lament King Henry's corse.

Enter *Richard, Duke of Gloucester.*

Rich. Stay, you that bear the corse, and set it down.
Anne. What black magician conjures up this fiend, 35
To stop devoted charitable deeds?
Rich. Villains, set down the corse, or, by Saint Paul,
I'll make a corse of him that disobeys!
Gent. My lord, stand back, and let the coffin pass.
Rich. Unmannered dog! Stand thou, when I command! 40
Advance thy halberd higher than my breast,
Or, by Saint Paul, I'll strike thee to my foot,
And spurn upon thee, beggar, for thy boldness.
[*The Bearers set down the hearse.*]

51. **curst:** shrewish; ill-tempered.
57. **pattern:** example.
61. **exhales:** brings forth.
68. **quick:** alive.

Henry VI.
From an 1811 reprint of John Rastell, *The Pastime of People* (1529).

Anne. What, do you tremble? Are you all afraid? 45
Alas, I blame you not, for you are mortal,
And mortal eyes cannot endure the Devil.
Avaunt, thou dreadful minister of hell!
Thou hadst but power over his mortal body;
His soul thou canst not have. Therefore, be gone. 50
Rich. Sweet saint, for charity, be not so curst.
Anne. Foul devil, for God's sake hence, and trouble us not,
For thou hast made the happy earth thy hell,
Filled it with cursing cries and deep exclaims. 55
If thou delight to view thy heinous deeds,
Behold this pattern of thy butcheries.
O gentlemen, see, see, dead Henry's wounds
Open their congealed mouths and bleed afresh!
Blush, blush, thou lump of foul deformity; 60
For 'tis thy presence that exhales this blood
From cold and empty veins where no blood dwells.
Thy deeds, inhuman and unnatural,
Provokes this deluge most unnatural.
O God, which this blood madest, revenge his death! 65
O earth, which this blood drinkst, revenge his death!
Either heav'n with lightning strike the murd'rer dead;
Or earth gape open wide and eat him quick,
As thou dost swallow up this good king's blood
Which his hell-governed arm hath butchered! 70
Rich. Lady, you know no rules of charity,
Which renders good for bad, blessings for curses.
Anne. Villain, thou knowst no law of God nor man:
No beast so fierce but knows some touch of pity.
Rich. But I know none, and therefore am no beast. 75

78-9. **Vouchsafe . . . to give me leave:** allow me.

80. **By circumstance:** by a detailed explanation.

81. **diffused:** distorted; deformed.

89. **current:** negotiable; i.e., no excuse which will pass.

102. **falchion:** sword.

Anne. O wonderful, when devils tell the truth!
Rich. More wonderful, when angels are so angry.
Vouchsafe, divine perfection of a woman,
Of these supposed crimes, to give me leave
By circumstance but to acquit myself. 80
Anne. Vouchsafe, diffused infection of a man,
Of these known evils, but to give me leave
By circumstance t'accuse thy cursed self.
Rich. Fairer than tongue can name thee, let me have 85
Some patient leisure to excuse myself.
Anne. Fouler than heart can think thee, thou canst make
No excuse current but to hang thyself.
Rich. By such despair I should accuse myself. 90
Anne. And by despairing shalt thou stand excused
For doing worthy vengeance on thyself
That didst unworthy slaughter upon others.
Rich. Say that I slew them not?
Anne. Then say they were not slain. 95
But dead they are, and, devilish slave, by thee.
Rich. I did not kill your husband.
Anne. Why, then he is alive.
Rich. Nay, he is dead, and slain by Edward's hands.
Anne. In thy foul throat thou liest! Queen Margaret saw 100
Thy murd'rous falchion smoking in his blood;
The which thou once didst bend against her breast,
But that thy brothers beat aside the point.
Rich. I was provoked by her sland'rous tongue, 105
That laid their guilt upon my guiltless shoulders.

119. **holp:** helped. This is the past tense of a strong verb form of "help," and until recently it was current in backwoods speech.

133. **timeless:** untimely.

137. **effect:** probably "effecter."

Anne. Thou wast provoked by thy bloody mind,
That never dreamst on aught but butcheries.
Didst thou not kill this king?

Rich. I grant ye. 110

Anne. Dost grant me, hedgehog? Then God grant me too
Thou mayst be damned for that wicked deed!
O, he was gentle, mild, and virtuous!

Rich. The better for the King of heaven that hath him. 115

Anne. He is in heaven, where thou shalt never come.

Rich. Let him thank me, that holp to send him thither; 120
For he was fitter for that place than earth.

Anne. And thou unfit for any place but hell.

Rich. Yes, one place else, if you will hear me name it.

Anne. Some dungeon. 125

Rich. Your bedchamber.

Anne. Ill rest betide the chamber where thou liest!

Rich. So will it, madam, till I lie with you.

Anne. I hope so.

Rich. I know so. But, gentle Lady Anne, 130
To leave this keen encounter of our wits
And fall something into a slower method;
Is not the causer of the timeless deaths
Of these Plantagenets, Henry and Edward,
As blameful as the executioner? 135

Anne. Thou wast the cause and most accursed effect.

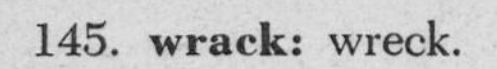

145. **wrack:** wreck.

Rich. Your beauty was the cause of that effect—
Your beauty, that did haunt me in my sleep
To undertake the death of all the world, 140
So I might live one hour in your sweet bosom.
Anne. If I thought that, I tell thee, homicide,
These nails should rent that beauty from my cheeks.
Rich. These eyes could not endure that beauty's wrack; 145
You should not blemish it, if I stood by:
As all the world is cheered by the sun,
So I by that. It is my day, my life.
Anne. Black night o'ershade thy day, and death thy life! 150
Rich. Curse not thyself, fair creature, thou art both.
Anne. I would I were, to be revenged on thee.
Rich. It is a quarrel most unnatural,
To be revenged on him that loveth thee. 155
Anne. It is a quarrel just and reasonable,
To be revenged on him that killed my husband.
Rich. He that bereft thee, lady, of thy husband,
Did it to help thee to a better husband.
Anne. His better doth not breathe upon the earth. 160
Rich. He lives that loves thee better than he could.
Anne. Name him.
Rich. Plantagenet.
Anne. Why, that was he.
Rich. The selfsame name, but one of better nature. 165
Anne. Where is he?
Rich. Here. ([*She*] *spits at him.*)
Why dost thou spit at me?

169. **mortal:** deadly.

174. **basilisks:** fabulous creatures with the power of death in their glances.

179. **aspects:** glances.

182. **Rutland:** Richard's brother Edmund, Earl of Rutland, who was killed in the same battle as their father.

190. **exhale:** draw forth; see l. 61.

193. **smoothing:** flattering.

194. **is proposed my fee:** is my promised reward.

A cockatrice or basilisk.
From Konrad Gesner, *Historiae animalium* (1585).

Anne. Would it were mortal poison, for thy sake!
Rich. Never came poison from so sweet a place. 170
Anne. Never hung poison on a fouler toad.
Out of my sight! Thou dost infect mine eyes.
Rich. Thine eyes, sweet lady, have infected mine.
Anne. Would they were basilisks, to strike thee dead! 175
Rich. I would they were, that I might die at once;
For now they kill me with a living death.
Those eyes of thine from mine have drawn salt tears,
Shamed their aspects with store of childish drops:
These eyes, which never shed remorseful tear, 180
No, when my father York and Edward wept
To hear the piteous moan that Rutland made
When black-faced Clifford shook his sword at him;
Nor when thy warlike father, like a child,
Told the sad story of my father's death, 185
And twenty times made pause to sob and weep,
That all the standers-by had wet their cheeks
Like trees bedashed with rain: in that sad time
My manly eyes did scorn an humble tear;
And what these sorrows could not thence exhale, 190
Thy beauty hath, and made them blind with weeping.
I never sued to friend nor enemy;
My tongue could never learn sweet smoothing word;
But, now thy beauty is proposed my fee,
My proud heart sues, and prompts my tongue to speak. 195

She looks scornfully at him.

Teach not thy lip such scorn, for it was made
For kissing, lady, not for such contempt.

S.D. after l. 209. **falls:** drops.

219. **accessary:** a variant spelling of "accessory."

221. **figured in my tongue:** portrayed exactly in what I say.

If thy revengeful heart cannot forgive,
Lo, here I lend thee this sharp-pointed sword, 200
Which if thou please to hide in this true breast,
And let the soul forth that adoreth thee,
I lay it naked to the deadly stroke,
And humbly beg the death upon my knee.
He lays his breast open. She offers at [*it*] *with his sword.*
Nay, do not pause: for I did kill King Henry— 205
But 'twas thy beauty that provoked me.
Nay, now dispatch: 'twas I that stabbed young Edward—
But 'twas thy heavenly face that set me on.
She falls the sword.
Take up the sword again, or take up me. 210
Anne. Arise, dissembler: though I wish thy death,
I will not be thy executioner.
Rich. Then bid me kill myself, and I will do it.
Anne. I have already.
Rich. That was in thy rage: 215
Speak it again, and even with the word,
This hand, which for thy love did kill thy love,
Shall for thy love kill a far truer love;
To both their deaths shalt thou be accessary.
Anne. I would I knew thy heart. 220
Rich. 'Tis figured in my tongue.
Anne. I fear me both are false.
Rich. Then never man was true.
Anne. Well, well, put up your sword.
Rich. Say, then, my peace is made. 225
Anne. That shalt thou know hereafter.

229. **Vouchsafe:** deign; see l. 78.

241. **presently repair:** immediately remove; **Crosby House:** Richard's town house, which then stood in Bishopsgate Street. It was later removed and re-erected in Chelsea, where it still stands.

245. **expedient:** speedy; expeditious.

Rich. But shall I live in hope?
Anne. All men, I hope, live so.
Rich. Vouchsafe to wear this ring.
Anne. To take is not to give. 230
[*Richard places a ring on her finger.*]
Rich. Look how my ring encompasseth thy finger,
Even so thy breast encloseth my poor heart:
Wear both of them, for both of them are thine.
And if thy poor devoted servant may
But beg one favor at thy gracious hand, 235
Thou dost confirm his happiness for ever.
Anne. What is it?
Rich. That it may please you leave these sad designs
To him that hath most cause to be a mourner, 240
And presently repair to Crosby House;
Where, after I have solemnly interred
At Chertsey monast'ry this noble king,
And wet his grave with my repentant tears,
I will with all expedient duty see you. 245
For divers unknown reasons, I beseech you,
Grant me this boon.
Anne. With all my heart; and much it joys me too,
To see you are become so penitent.
Tressel and Berkeley, go along with me. 250
Rich. Bid me farewell.
Anne. 'Tis more than you deserve;
But since you teach me how to flatter you,
Imagine I have said farewell already.
Exeunt two with Anne.
Rich. Sirs, take up the corse. 255

268. **the plain Devil:** merely the Devil.

269. **all the world to nothing:** despite all the world.

272. **since:** ago.

275. **Framed in the prodigality of nature:** naturally endowed with abundant virtues.

278. **abase:** lower.

279. **cropped:** cut off; **prime:** springtime; i.e., youth.

281. **moiety:** half.

283. **My dukedom to a beggarly denier:** that is, I'll bet my dukedom against a single coin of the lowest value. A **denier** was a copper coin worth only about a tenth of an English penny of the time.

A nobleman of the reign of Edward IV.
From a costume design by J. R. Planché (1829).

Gent. Towards Chertsey, noble lord?
Rich. No, to Whitefriars; there attend my coming.
Exit [Bearers and Guard with] Corse.
Was ever woman in this humor wooed?
Was ever woman in this humor won?
I'll have her, but I will not keep her long. 260
What! I, that killed her husband and his father,
To take her in her heart's extremest hate,
With curses in her mouth, tears in her eyes,
The bleeding witness of my hatred by,
Having God, her conscience, and these bars against me, 265
And I no friends to back my suit withal
But the plain Devil and dissembling looks,
And yet to win her, all the world to nothing!
Ha! 270
Hath she forgot already that brave prince,
Edward, her lord, whom I, some three months since,
Stabbed in my angry mood at Tewkesbury?
A sweeter and a lovelier gentleman,
Framed in the prodigality of nature— 275
Young, valiant, wise, and, no doubt, right royal—
The spacious world cannot again afford;
And will she yet abase her eyes on me,
That cropped the golden prime of this sweet prince
And made her widow to a woeful bed? 280
On me, whose all not equals Edward's moiety?
On me, that halts and am misshapen thus?
My dukedom to a beggarly denier,
I do mistake my person all this while!
Upon my life, she finds, although I cannot, 285

286. **marv'lous proper:** wonderfully handsome.
287. **be at charges for:** stand the expense of.
288. **entertain:** retain; hire.
292. **in:** into.

I. iii. Queen Elizabeth is distressed at the King's illness and the fact that his brother Richard will be Protector to her son if the King dies. The Earls of Buckingham and Derby give a hopeful report of the King's state of mind and summon the Queen to meet with Richard and Lord Hastings in the King's presence so that he may reconcile them. Richard appears and complains that he has been slandered to the King, implying that the Queen is responsible and also accusing her of wishing the death of Clarence. Margaret of Anjou, widow of Henry VI, then comes in and upbraids all those present for the wrongs done to her in depriving her of her crown; she blames Richard in particular for the murder of her son and husband.

When the rest have departed to answer the King's summons, Richard confers with two murderers, whom he sends to the Tower to kill Clarence.

4. **brook:** tolerate; see I. i. 136.
7. **betide on:** befall; see I. ii. 18.
11-2. **a goodly son:** Prince Edward, called Edward V, who was, presumably, murdered in the Tower on Richard's order.

Myself to be a marv'lous proper man.
I'll be at charges for a looking glass
And entertain a score or two of tailors
To study fashions to adorn my body:
Since I am crept in favor with myself, 290
I will maintain it with some little cost.
But first I'll turn yon fellow in his grave,
And then return lamenting to my love.
Shine out, fair sun, till I have bought a glass,
That I may see my shadow as I pass. 295

Exit.

Scene III. [London. The Palace.]

Enter the *Queen Mother* [*Elizabeth*], *Lord Rivers,* and *Lord Grey* [with the *Marquess of Dorset*].

Riv. Have patience, madam; there's no doubt his Majesty
Will soon recover his accustomed health.
Grey. In that you brook it ill, it makes him worse:
Therefore, for God's sake, entertain good comfort 5
And cheer his Grace with quick and merry eyes.
Queen. If he were dead, what would betide on me?
Grey. No other harm but loss of such a lord.
Queen. The loss of such a lord includes all harms. 10
Grey. The heavens have blessed you with a goodly son,
To be your comforter when he is gone.
Queen. Ah, he is young, and his minority

15. **put unto the trust of Richard Gloucester:** by the terms of Edward IV's will, Richard was to be Protector of the realm until the Prince of Wales came of age.

18. **determined, not concluded:** that is, the decision has been reached but no official decree has been made.

19. **miscarry:** die.

Ent. after l. 19. **Derby:** Thomas, Lord Stanley, created Earl of Derby after the Battle of Bosworth Field. Shakespeare is anticipating his elevation to an earldom.

25. **Countess Richmond:** Margaret Beaufort, great-granddaughter of John of Gaunt and mother of Henry VII. The title Countess of Richmond comes from her first marriage to Edmund Tudor, Earl of Richmond, son of Katherine Valois and Owen Tudor. From this ancestry Henry VII received a double claim to the English crown, though flawed by illegitimacy on both sides. It was later claimed that Owen Tudor was descended from Cadwallader, last British King of Wales.

32. **envious:** malicious.

35. **From wayward sickness, and no grounded malice:** that is, from an uncontrollable malady, not from reasoned ill will.

38. **But:** just.

Is put unto the trust of Richard Gloucester, 15
A man that loves not me, nor none of you.
Riv. Is it concluded he shall be Protector?
Queen. It is determined, not concluded yet:
But so it must be, if the King miscarry.

Enter *Buckingham* and [*Stanley, Earl of*] *Derby.*

Grey. Here come the lords of Buckingham and Derby. 20
Buck. Good time of day unto your royal Grace!
Der. God make your Majesty joyful as you have been!
Queen. The Countess Richmond, good my Lord of Derby, 25
To your good prayer will scarcely say "Amen."
Yet, Derby, notwithstanding she's your wife
And loves not me, be you, good lord, assured
I hate not you for her proud arrogance. 30
Der. I do beseech you, either not believe
The envious slanders of her false accusers;
Or, if she be accused on true report,
Bear with her weakness, which I think proceeds
From wayward sickness, and no grounded malice. 35
Queen. Saw you the King today, my Lord of Derby?
Der. But now the Duke of Buckingham and I
Are come from visiting his Majesty.
Queen. What likelihood of his amendment, lords? 40
Buck. Madam, good hope; his Grace speaks cheerfully.

45. **make atonement:** bring about a reconciliation.

48. **warn:** summon.

58. **smooth:** flatter; see I. ii. 193; **cog:** cheat.

59. **French nods:** affected gestures. Many contemporary writers were fond of deriding the polite fashions imported from France.

60. **held:** regarded as.

63. **Jacks:** base fellows; knaves.

66. **grace:** virtue.

Queen. God grant him health! Did you confer with him?

Buck. Ay, madam: he desires to make atonement 45
Between the Duke of Gloucester and your brothers,
And between them and my Lord Chamberlain,
And sent to warn them to his royal presence.

Queen. Would all were well! but that will never be: 50
I fear our happiness is at the height.

Enter *Richard* [and *Lord Hastings*].

Rich. They do me wrong, and I will not endure it!
Who is it that complains unto the King
That I, forsooth, am stern, and love them not?
By holy Paul, they love his Grace but lightly 55
That fill his ears with such dissentious rumors.
Because I cannot flatter and look fair,
Smile in men's faces, smooth, deceive, and cog,
Duck with French nods and apish courtesy,
I must be held a rancorous enemy. 60
Cannot a plain man live and think no harm,
But thus his simple truth must be abused
With silken, sly, insinuating Jacks?

Grey. To who in all this presence speaks your Grace? 65

Rich. To thee, that hast nor honesty nor grace.
When have I injured thee? when done thee wrong?
Or thee? or thee? or any of your faction?
A plague upon you all! His royal Grace,
Whom God preserve better than you would wish! 70

71. **a breathing-while:** the space of a breath.

72. **lewd:** vicious; wicked.

95. **a noble:** a coin, with a play on "noble person."

96. **careful:** the literal meaning: full of care.

98. **hap:** fortune; see I. ii. 18.

Cannot be quiet scarce a breathing-while
But you must trouble him with lewd complaints.

Queen. Brother of Gloucester, you mistake the matter:
The King, on his own royal disposition, 75
And not provoked by any suitor else,
Aiming, belike, at your interior hatred,
That in your outward action shows itself
Against my children, brothers, and myself,
Makes him to send, that he may learn the ground. 80

Rich. I cannot tell: the world is grown so bad
That wrens make prey where eagles dare not perch.
Since every Jack became a gentleman,
There's many a gentle person made a Jack.

Queen. Come, come, we know your meaning, brother Gloucester: 85
You envy my advancement and my friends'.
God grant we never may have need of you!

Rich. Meantime, God grants that I have need of you. 90
Our brother is imprisoned by your means,
Myself disgraced, and the nobility
Held in contempt, while great promotions
Are daily given to ennoble those
That scarce, some two days since, were worth a noble. 95

Queen. By Him that raised me to this careful height
From that contented hap which I enjoyed,
I never did incense his Majesty
Against the Duke of Clarence, but have been 100
An earnest advocate to plead for him.

103. **draw me in these vile suspects:** i.e., involve me in these vile suspicions.

113. **marry:** an oath with the force of "indeed." Here there is a pun on the meaning "wed."

117. **Iwis:** certainly, from the Old English *gewis;* **your grandam had a worser match:** i.e., Jacquetta, Duchess of Bedford, who married Richard Woodville, a mere squire and therefore of lower birth than herself.

Ent. after l. 125. **Queen Margaret:** Actually Margaret of Anjou was captured by Edward IV at the Battle of Tewkesbury and ransomed by King Louis of France, and she remained in France from about 1476 until her death in 1482. Thus, historically she was not in England and could not have appeared in the scenes where Shakespeare places her.

129. **is due to me:** i.e., are rightfully mine.

My lord, you do me shameful injury
Falsely to draw me in these vile suspects.
Rich. You may deny that you were not the mean
Of my Lord Hastings' late imprisonment. 105
Riv. She may, my lord, for—
Rich. She may, Lord Rivers! Why, who knows not so?
She may do more, sir, than denying that:
She may help you to many fair preferments, 110
And then deny her aiding hand therein
And lay those honors on your high desert.
What may she not? She may, ay, marry, may she.
Riv. What, marry, may she?
Rich. What, marry, may she? Marry with a king, 115
A bachelor and a handsome stripling too:
Iwis your grandam had a worser match.
Queen. My Lord of Gloucester, I have too long borne
Your blunt upbraidings and your bitter scoffs: 120
By heaven, I will acquaint his Majesty
Of those gross taunts that oft I have endured.
I had rather be a country servant maid
Than a great queen with this condition,
To be so baited, scorned, and stormed at: 125

Enter *Old Queen Margaret,* [unnoticed].

Small joy have I in being England's queen.
Queen M. [*Aside*] And lessened be that small, God I beseech Him!
Thy honor, state, and seat is due to me.

135. **pains:** former efforts on the King's behalf.

142. **pack horse:** drudge.

149. **Were factious for:** supported.

151. **Margaret's battle at St. Albans:** the Battle of St. Albans between the Yorkists and Lancastrians, February 17, 1461.

157. **father:** father-in-law; Clarence had married Warwick's daughter Isabel.

Rich. What? Threat you me with telling of the King? 130
Tell him, and spare not. Look, what I have said
I will avouch't in presence of the King:
I dare adventure to be sent to the Tower.
'Tis time to speak: my pains are quite forgot. 135

Queen M. [*Aside*] Out, devil! I do remember them too well:
Thou kill'dst my husband Henry in the Tower,
And Edward, my poor son, at Tewkesbury.

Rich. Ere you were Queen, ay, or your husband King, 140
I was a pack horse in his great affairs;
A weeder-out of his proud adversaries,
A liberal rewarder of his friends:
To royalize his blood I spent mine own. 145

Queen M. [*Aside*] Ay, and much better blood than his or thine.

Rich. In all which time you and your husband Grey
Were factious for the house of Lancaster;
And, Rivers, so were you. Was not your husband 150
In Margaret's battle at St. Albans slain?
Let me put in your minds, if you forget,
What you have been ere this, and what you are;
Withal, what I have been, and what I am.

Queen M. [*Aside*] A murd'rous villain, and so still thou art. 155

Rich. Poor Clarence did forsake his father, Warwick;
Ay, and forswore himself, which Jesu pardon!

Queen M. [*Aside*] Which God revenge! 160

162. **meed:** reward.

168. **cacodemon:** evil spirit.

170. **urge:** mention.

184. **pilled:** pillaged; stolen.

188. **gentle villain:** a play on words. **Villain** often meant the opposite of **gentle,** that is, lowborn, but to Margaret, Richard is a gently-born rascal.

189-90. **what makest thou in my sight:** what are you doing here.

Rich. To fight on Edward's party for the crown;
And for his meed, poor lord, he is mewed up.
I would to God my heart were flint like Edward's,
Or Edward's soft and pitiful like mine:
I am too childish-foolish for this world. 165

Queen M. [*Aside*] Hie thee to hell for shame, and leave this world,
Thou cacodemon! there thy kingdom is.

Riv. My Lord of Gloucester, in those busy days
Which here you urge to prove us enemies, 170
We followed then our lord, our sovereign king.
So should we you, if you should be our king.

Rich. If I should be? I had rather be a peddler:
Far be it from my heart, the thought thereof!

Queen. As little joy, my lord, as you suppose 175
You should enjoy, were you this country's king,
As little joy you may suppose in me
That I enjoy, being the queen thereof.

Queen M. [*Aside*] A little joy enjoys the queen thereof; 180
For I am she, and altogether joyless.
I can no longer hold me patient. [*Advancing.*]
Hear me, you wrangling pirates, that fall out
In sharing that which you have pilled from me!
Which of you trembles not that looks on me? 185
If not, that I am Queen, you bow like subjects,
Yet that, by you deposed, you quake like rebels?
Ah, gentle villain, do not turn away!

Rich. Foul wrinkled witch, what makest thou in my sight? 190

204. **clout:** cloth.

208. **plagued:** punished.

210. **that babe:** actually, Edmund was sixteen at the time of his death.

Queen M. But repetition of what thou hast marred:
That will I make before I let thee go.
Rich. Wert thou not banished on pain of death?
Queen M. I was; but I do find more pain in banishment 195
Than death can yield me here by my abode.
A husband and a son thou owest to me—
And thou a kingdom—all of you allegiance.
This sorrow that I have, by right is yours,
And all the pleasures you usurp are mine. 200
Rich. The curse my noble father laid on thee,
When thou didst crown his warlike brows with paper,
And with thy scorns drewst rivers from his eyes,
And then, to dry them, gavest the Duke a clout
Steeped in the faultless blood of pretty Rutland— 205
His curses then, from bitterness of soul
Denounced against thee, are all fall'n upon thee;
And God, not we, hath plagued thy bloody deed.
Queen. So just is God, to right the innocent.
Hast. O, 'twas the foulest deed to slay that babe, 210
And the most merciless, that e'er was heard of!
Riv. Tyrants themselves wept when it was reported.
Dor. No man but prophesied revenge for it.
Buck. Northumberland, then present, wept to see it. 215
Queen M. What? were you snarling all before I came,
Ready to catch each other by the throat,
And turn you all your hatred now on me? 220
Did York's dread curse prevail so much with heaven

226. **quick:** vital; see I. ii. 68.
236. **stalled:** installed.

Edward IV and Prince Edward.
From a costume design by J. R. Planché (1829).

That Henry's death, my lovely Edward's death,
Their kingdom's loss, my woeful banishment,
Should all but answer for that peevish brat?
Can curses pierce the clouds and enter heaven? 225
Why then, give way, dull clouds, to my quick curses!
Though not by war, by surfeit die your king,
As ours by murder, to make him a king!
Edward thy son, that now is Prince of Wales,
For Edward our son, that was Prince of Wales, 230
Die in his youth by like untimely violence!
Thyself a queen, for me that was a queen,
Outlive thy glory, like my wretched self!
Long mayst thou live to wail thy children's death
And see another, as I see thee now, 235
Decked in thy rights, as thou art stalled in mine!
Long die thy happy days before thy death,
And, after many lengthened hours of grief,
Die neither mother, wife, nor England's Queen!
Rivers and Dorset, you were standers-by, 240
And so wast thou, Lord Hastings, when my son
Was stabbed with bloody daggers: God I pray Him
That none of you may live his natural age,
But by some unlooked accident cut off!

Rich. Have done thy charm, thou hateful withered hag! 245

Queen M. And leave out thee? Stay, dog, for thou shalt hear me.

If heaven have any grievous plague in store
Exceeding those that I can wish upon thee, 250
O let them keep it till thy sins be ripe,
And then hurl down their indignation

255. **suspect:** suspected.

260. **elvish-marked:** i.e., marked by elves; deformed; **hog:** a reference to the symbol of a boar, which Richard had taken as his badge.

261-62. **sealed . . . The slave of nature:** branded at birth one of nature's inferior creatures.

270. **cry thee mercy:** beg your pardon.

273. **period:** conclusion.

277. **painted queen:** i.e., a queen only in show, not truly queenly by nature; **flourish:** ornament. Queen Elizabeth is compared to a mere picture illustrating how a queen should look.

279. **bottled:** swollen.

283. **bunch-backed:** humpbacked.

On thee, the troubler of the poor world's peace!
The worm of conscience still begnaw thy soul!
Thy friends suspect for traitors while thou livest, 255
And take deep traitors for thy dearest friends!
No sleep close up that deadly eye of thine,
Unless it be while some tormenting dream
Affrights thee with a hell of ugly devils!
Thou elvish-marked, abortive, rooting hog! 260
Thou that wast sealed in thy nativity
The slave of nature and the son of hell!
Thou slander of thy heavy mother's womb!
Thou loathed issue of thy father's loins!
Thou rag of honor! thou detested– 265

Rich. Margaret.

Queen M. Richard!

Rich. Ha!

Queen M. I call thee not.

Rich. I cry thee mercy then; for I did think 270
That thou hadst called me all these bitter names.

Queen M. Why, so I did, but looked for no reply.
O let me make the period to my curse!

Rich. 'Tis done by me, and ends in "Margaret."

Queen. Thus have you breathed your curse against yourself. 275

Queen M. Poor painted queen, vain flourish of my fortune!
Why strewst thou sugar on that bottled spider,
Whose deadly web ensnareth thee about? 280
Fool, fool! thou whetst a knife to kill thyself.
The day will come that thou shalt wish for me
To help thee curse this poisonous bunch-backed toad.

284. **False-boding:** uttering false prophecies; **frantic:** frenzied.

288. **well:** that is, appropriately.

295-96. **malapert:** impertinent; saucy.

297. **fire-new:** i.e., freshly minted.

306. **eyrie:** eagle's brood.

313. **suffer:** allow.

Hast. False-boding woman, end thy frantic curse,
Lest to thy harm thou move our patience. 285
Queen M. Foul shame upon you! you have all moved mine.
Riv. Were you well served, you would be taught your duty.
Queen M. To serve me well, you all should do me duty, 290
Teach me to be your queen, and you my subjects:
O serve me well, and teach yourselves that duty!
Dor. Dispute not with her; she is lunatic.
Queen M. Peace, Master Marquess, you are malapert: 295
Your fire-new stamp of honor is scarce current.
O that your young nobility could judge
What 'twere to lose it and be miserable!
They that stand high have many blasts to shake them, 300
And if they fall, they dash themselves to pieces.
Rich. Good counsel, marry! Learn it, learn it, Marquess.
Dor. It touches you, my lord, as much as me.
Rich. Ay, and much more; but I was born so high: 305
Our eyrie buildeth in the cedar's top,
And dallies with the wind and scorns the sun.
Queen M. And turns the sun to shade—alas! alas!
Witness my son, now in the shade of death,
Whose bright outshining beams thy cloudy wrath 310
Hath in eternal darkness folded up.
Your eyrie buildeth in our eyrie's nest:
O God, that seest it, do not suffer it!
As it is won with blood, lost be it so!

Lady of the reign of Richard III.
From a costume design by J. R. Planché (1829).

Buck. Peace, peace, for shame, if not for charity. 315
Queen M. Urge neither charity nor shame to me:
[*To the others*] Uncharitably with me have you dealt,
And shamefully my hopes by you are butchered.
My charity is outrage, life my shame,
And in that shame still live my sorrow's rage! 320
Buck. Have done, have done.
Queen M. O princely Buckingham, I'll kiss thy hand
In sign of league and amity with thee:
Now fair befall thee and thy noble house! 325
Thy garments are not spotted with our blood,
Nor thou within the compass of my curse.
Buck. Nor no one here; for curses never pass
The lips of those that breathe them in the air.
Queen M. I will not think but they ascend the sky 330
And there awake God's gentle-sleeping peace.
O Buckingham, take heed of yonder dog!
Look, when he fawns he bites; and when he bites,
His venom tooth will rankle to the death.
Have not to do with him, beware of him: 335
Sin, death, and hell have set their marks on him,
And all their ministers attend on him.
Rich. What doth she say, my Lord of Buckingham?
Buck. Nothing that I respect, my gracious lord.
Queen M. What, dost thou scorn me for my gentle counsel? 340
And soothe the devil that I warn thee from?
O, but remember this another day,
When he shall split thy very heart with sorrow,
And say poor Margaret was a prophetess! 345

348. **an:** on.

349. **muse:** wonder.

354. **vantage:** advantage.

355-56. **too hot to do somebody good/ That is too cold in thinking of it now:** too eager to help Edward, who is now coldly ungrateful.

358. **franked up to fatting:** enclosed in a **frank** (sty) to be fattened for killing.

361. **scathe:** harm.

371. **set abroach:** loose; set afoot. The metaphor is from opening the tap of a barrel of drink.

372. **lay unto the grievous charge of others:** blame others severely for.

Live each of you the subjects to his hate,
And he to yours, and all of you to God's! *Exit.*
Buck. My hair doth stand an end to hear her curses.
Riv. And so doth mine. I muse why she's at liberty.
Rich. I cannot blame her. By God's holy Mother, 350
She hath had too much wrong, and I repent
My part thereof that I have done to her.
Queen. I never did her any, to my knowledge.
Rich. Yet you have all the vantage of her wrong:
I was too hot to do somebody good 355
That is too cold in thinking of it now.
Marry, as for Clarence, he is well repaid:
He is franked up to fatting for his pains.
God pardon them that are the cause thereof!
Riv. A virtuous and a Christianlike conclusion, 360
To pray for them that have done scathe to us.
Rich. So do I ever—(*Speaks to himself*) being well advised;
For had I cursed now, I had cursed myself.

Enter *Catesby.*

Cates. Madam, his Majesty doth call for you; 365
And for your Grace; and yours, my gracious lord.
Queen. Catesby, I come. Lords, will you go with me?
Riv. We wait upon your Grace.
Exeunt all but [*Richard of*] *Gloucester.*
Rich. I do the wrong, and first begin to brawl. 370
The secret mischiefs that I set abroach
I lay unto the grievous charge of others.

374. **gulls:** fools.
383. **odd old ends:** scraps.
386. **resolved:** resolute.
396. **mark:** heed.
398. **prate:** chatter.

Clarence, who I, indeed, have cast in darkness,
I do beweep to many simple gulls—
Namely, to Derby, Hastings, Buckingham— 375
And tell them 'tis the Queen and her allies
That stir the King against the Duke my brother.
Now they believe it, and withal whet me
To be revenged on Rivers, Dorset, Grey.
But then I sigh, and, with a piece of Scripture, 380
Tell them that God bids us do good for evil:
And thus I clothe my naked villainy
With odd old ends stol'n forth of Holy Writ,
And seem a saint, when most I play the Devil.

Enter *Two Murderers.*

But soft! Here come my executioners. 385
How now, my hardy, stout, resolved mates!
Are you now going to dispatch this thing?
1. Mur. We are, my lord, and come to have the warrant,
That we may be admitted where he is. 390
Rich. Well thought upon; I have it here about me:
[*Gives the warrant.*]
When you have done, repair to Crosby Place.
But, sirs, be sudden in the execution,
Withal obdurate, do not hear him plead;
For Clarence is well-spoken, and perhaps 395
May move your hearts to pity if you mark him.
1. Mur. Tut, tut, my lord! we will not stand to prate;

403. **straight:** at once.

I. iv. Clarence tells his keeper of a dreadful dream he has had, in which he was lured by Richard to a watery death. The two murderers enter and Clarence realizes that they mean to kill him. They report that the King has ordered his death, but when he pleads with them and promises a reward from his brother Richard if they spare him, they reveal that Richard has hired them. They stab Clarence and drag him away to drown in a butt of malmsey wine.

---

1. **heavily:** sadly.
15. **hatches:** decks.

Talkers are no good doers. Be assured:
We go to use our hands, and not our tongues. 400
Rich. Your eyes drop millstones, when fools' eyes fall tears.
I like you, lads: about your business straight.
Go, go, dispatch.
1. Mur. We will, my noble lord. 405
Exeunt.

Scene IV. [London. The Tower.]

Enter *Clarence* and *Keeper*.

Keep. Why looks your Grace so heavily today?
Clar. O, I have passed a miserable night,
So full of fearful dreams, of ugly sights,
That, as I am a Christian faithful man,
I would not spend another such a night 5
Though 'twere to buy a world of happy days,
So full of dismal terror was the time.
Keep. What was your dream, my lord? I pray you tell me.
Clar. Methoughts that I had broken from the Tower, 10
And was embarked to cross to Burgundy,
And in my company my brother Gloucester,
Who from my cabin tempted me to walk
Upon the hatches: thence we looked toward England 15
And cited up a thousand heavy times,
During the wars of York and Lancaster,
That had befall'n us. As we paced along

21. **stay:** hold.

29. **Inestimable:** impossible to estimate; numberless; **unvalued:** invaluable; priceless.

39. **yield:** i.e., give up.

41. **vast:** desolate and endless.

42. **bulk:** body; no reference to his size is intended.

44. **sore:** grievous; extreme.

47-8. **melancholy flood:** the River Styx of the classical underworld. The **ferryman** is Charon, who carried spirits across the river, never to return.

Upon the giddy footing of the hatches,
Methought that Gloucester stumbled, and in falling 20
Struck me, that thought to stay him, overboard,
Into the tumbling billows of the main.
O Lord! methought what pain it was to drown!
What dreadful noise of waters in mine ears!
What sights of ugly death within mine eyes! 25
Methoughts I saw a thousand fearful wracks;
A thousand men that fishes gnawed upon;
Wedges of gold, great anchors, heaps of pearl,
Inestimable stones, unvalued jewels,
All scatt'red in the bottom of the sea: 30
Some lay in dead men's skulls, and in the holes
Where eyes did once inhabit, there were crept,
As 'twere in scorn of eyes, reflecting gems,
That wooed the slimy bottom of the deep,
And mocked the dead bones that lay scatt'red by. 35

Keep. Had you such leisure in the time of death
To gaze upon these secrets of the deep?

Clar. Methought I had; and often did I strive
To yield the ghost; but still the envious flood
Stopped in my soul, and would not let it forth 40
To find the empty, vast, and wand'ring air,
But smothered it within my panting bulk,
Which almost burst to belch it in the sea.

Keep. Awaked you not in this sore agony?

Clar. No, no, my dream was lengthened after life. 45
O, then began the tempest to my soul!
I passed, methought, the melancholy flood,
With that sour ferryman which poets write of,

52. **perjury:** breaking an oath. Clarence at one time joined his father-in-law, the Earl of Warwick, in supporting the Lancastrian cause, but was later reconciled to his brother; see II. i. 117-18.

55. **A shadow like an angel:** this must be the youthful Edward, son of Henry VI, though Gloucester has already stated that he killed him. Shakespeare probably accepted Holinshed's version of how the prince died, which described his death as the combined responsibility of Richard, Clarence, Hastings, and Dorset, all of whom fell upon him when he was brought a prisoner before the King.

57. **fleeting:** fickle.

66. **though:** if.

70. **requites:** rewards.

76. **heavy:** sorrowful; see l. 1; **fain would:** would like to.

Unto the kingdom of perpetual night.
The first that there did greet my stranger-soul 50
Was my great father-in-law, renownèd Warwick,
Who spake aloud, "What scourge for perjury
Can this dark monarchy afford false Clarence?"
And so he vanished. Then came wand'ring by
A shadow like an angel, with bright hair 55
Dabbled in blood, and he shrieked out aloud,
"Clarence is come—false, fleeting, perjured Clarence,
That stabbed me in the field by Tewkesbury:
Seize on him, Furies, take him unto torment!"
With that, methought, a legion of foul fiends 60
Environed me, and howlèd in mine ears
Such hideous cries, that with the very noise
I, trembling, waked, and for a season after
Could not believe but that I was in hell,
Such terrible impression made my dream. 65

Keep. No marvel, lord, though it affrighted you;
I am afraid, methinks, to hear you tell it.

Clar. Ah, Keeper, Keeper, I have done these things,
That now give evidence against my soul,
For Edward's sake, and see how he requites me! 70
O God! if my deep prayers cannot appease Thee,
But Thou wilt be avenged on my misdeeds,
Yet execute Thy wrath in me alone:
O spare my guiltless wife and my poor children!
Keeper, I prithee sit by me awhile. 75
My soul is heavy, and I fain would sleep.

Keep. I will, my lord. God give your Grace good rest! [*Clarence sleeps.*]

79. **breaks seasons and reposing hours:** disrupts the normal course of the seasons and the periods set aside for sleep.

83. **for unfelt imaginations:** i.e., in exchange for intangible and unreal honors.

86. **fame:** reputation.

100. **to:** some verb such as "go" is understood in a construction like this.

Enter *Brakenbury*, the *Lieutenant.*

Brak. Sorrow breaks seasons and reposing hours,
Makes the night morning and the noontide night: 80
Princes have but their titles for their glories,
An outward honor for an inward toil;
And, for unfelt imaginations,
They often feel a world of restless cares;
So that between their titles and low name 85
There's nothing differs but the outward fame.

Enter *Two Murderers.*

1. Mur. Ho! who's here?

Brak. What wouldst thou, fellow? And how camest thou hither?

1. Mur. I would speak with Clarence, and I came 90
hither on my legs.

Brak. What, so brief?

2. Mur. 'Tis better, sir, than to be tedious. Let him see our commission, and talk no more.

[*Brakenbury*] *reads* [*it*].

Brak. I am, in this, commanded to deliver 95
The noble Duke of Clarence to your hands.
I will not reason what is meant hereby,
Because I will be guiltless from the meaning.
There lies the Duke asleep, and there the keys.
I'll to the King and signify to him 100
That thus I have resigned to you my charge.

111. **urging:** mention; see I. iii. 170.
121-22. **passionate humor:** compassionate mood.

The Furies.
From Vincenzo Cartari, *Imagini de gli dei delli antichi* (1615).
(See I. iv. 59.)

1. Mur. You may, sir; 'tis a point of wisdom. Fare you well.

Exit [Brakenbury with Keeper].

2. Mur. What? Shall we stab him as he sleeps?

1. Mur. No. He'll say 'twas done cowardly, when he wakes. 105

2. Mur. Why, he shall never wake until the great Judgment Day.

1. Mur. Why, then he'll say we stabbed him sleeping. 110

2. Mur. The urging of that word "judgment" hath bred a kind of remorse in me.

1. Mur. What? Art thou afraid?

2. Mur. Not to kill him, having a warrant; but to be damned for killing him, from the which no warrant can defend me. 115

1. Mur. I thought thou hadst been resolute.

2. Mur. So I am, to let him live.

1. Mur. I'll back to the Duke of Gloucester and tell him so. 120

2. Mur. Nay, I prithee stay a little. I hope this passionate humor of mine will change. It was wont to hold me but while one tells twenty.

1. Mur. How dost thou feel thyself now?

2. Mur. Some certain dregs of conscience are yet within me. 125

1. Mur. Remember our reward when the deed's done.

2. Mur. Come, he dies! I had forgot the reward.

1. Mur. Where's thy conscience now? 130

2. Mur. O, in the Duke of Gloucester's purse.

135. **entertain:** i.e., few would want to keep a conscience.

150-52. **Take the Devil in thy mind, and believe him not. He would insinuate with thee but to make thee sigh:** i.e., reason with your conscience and do not yield to its voice, for succumbing to remorse will only cause you misery. Conscience is portrayed as tempting to remorse, as the Devil tempts to sin.

155. **tall:** stout; valiant.

157. **Take him:** strike him; **costard:** a slang term for "head"; **hilts:** "hilt" often appeared in plural form because it was divided into two parts by the blade of the sword.

160. **sop:** a morsel of cake or bread, such as was used to dip in wine. There also may be a pun on the meaning "something of little value."

1. Mur. When he opens his purse to give us our reward, thy conscience flies out.

2. Mur. 'Tis no matter; let it go. There's few or none will entertain it. 135

1. Mur. What if it come to thee again?

2. Mur. I'll not meddle with it; it makes a man a coward. A man cannot steal, but it accuseth him; a man cannot swear, but it checks him; a man cannot lie with his neighbor's wife, but it detects him. 'Tis a 140 blushing shamefaced spirit that mutinies in a man's bosom. It fills a man full of obstacles. It made me once restore a purse of gold that by chance I found. It beggars any man that keeps it. It is turned out of towns and cities for a dangerous thing, and every 145 man that means to live well endeavors to trust to himself and live without it.

1. Mur. 'Tis even now at my elbow, persuading me not to kill the Duke.

2. Mur. Take the Devil in thy mind, and believe 150 him not. He would insinuate with thee but to make thee sigh.

1. Mur. I am strong-framed; he cannot prevail with me.

2. Mur. Spoke like a tall man that respects thy 155 reputation. Come, shall we fall to work?

1. Mur. Take him on the costard with the hilts of thy sword, and then throw him into the malmsey butt in the next room.

2. Mur. O excellent device! and make a sop of him. 160

1. Mur. Soft! he wakes.

2. Mur. Strike!

163. **reason:** talk.

171-72. **thy looks are humble:** that is, they look like men of low birth.

175. **deadly:** in a deadly manner; like the voice of death.

190. **quest:** inquest; i.e., a body of men set to decide the question.

193. **convict:** convicted. The final ending of the past tense of verbs was sometimes dropped for the sake of sound; see **suspect,** I. iii. 255.

1. Mur. No, we'll reason with him.
Clar. Where art thou, Keeper? Give me a cup of wine. 165
2. Mur. You shall have wine enough, my lord, anon.
Clar. In God's name, what art thou?
1. Mur. A man, as you are.
Clar. But not as I am, royal.
1. Mur. Nor you as we are, loyal. 170
Clar. Thy voice is thunder, but thy looks are humble.
1. Mur. My voice is now the King's, my looks mine own.
Clar. How darkly and how deadly dost thou speak! 175
Your eyes do menace me. Why look you pale?
Who sent you hither? Wherefore do you come?
Both. To, to, to—
Clar. To murder me?
Both. Ay, ay. 180
Clar. You scarcely have the hearts to tell me so,
And therefore cannot have the hearts to do it.
Wherein, my friends, have I offended you?
1. Mur. Offended us you have not, but the King.
Clar. I shall be reconciled to him again. 185
2. Mur. Never, my lord; therefore prepare to die.
Clar. Are you drawn forth among a world of men
To slay the innocent? What is my offense?
Where is the evidence that doth accuse me?
What lawful quest have given their verdict up 190
Unto the frowning judge? Or who pronounced
The bitter sentence of poor Clarence' death?
Before I be convict by course of law,

205-6. **vengeance . . . To hurl upon their heads:** i.e., thunderbolts.

219. **in such dear degree:** in a case of such extreme seriousness.

To threaten me with death is most unlawful:
I charge you, as you hope to have redemption 195
By Christ's dear blood shed for our grievous sins,
That you depart, and lay no hands on me.
The deed you undertake is damnable.

1. Mur. What we will do, we do upon command.

2. Mur. And he that hath commanded is our king. 200

Clar. Erroneous vassals! the great King of Kings
Hath in the table of His law commanded
That thou shalt do no murder. Will you then
Spurn at His edict, and fulfill a man's?
Take heed; for He holds vengeance in His hand 205
To hurl upon their heads that break His law.

2. Mur. And that same vengeance doth He hurl on thee
For false forswearing and for murder too:
Thou didst receive the sacrament to fight 210
In quarrel of the house of Lancaster.

1. Mur. And like a traitor to the name of God
Didst break that vow, and with thy treacherous blade
Unripst the bowels of thy sov'reign's son.

2. Mur. Whom thou wast sworn to cherish and defend. 215

1. Mur. How canst thou urge God's dreadful law to us,
When thou hast broke it in such dear degree?

Clar. Alas! for whose sake did I that ill deed? 220
For Edward, for my brother, for his sake.
He sends you not to murder me for this,
For in that sin he is as deep as I.
If God will be avenged for the deed,

227. **indirect:** roundabout.

230. **gallant-springing:** gallant in youth; showing youthful promise of nobility.

251. **lessoned:** instructed.

252. **kind:** natural in brotherly love, and virtuous.

253. **Right, as snow in harvest:** as natural as snow in harvesttime.

O know you yet, He doth it publicly! 225
Take not the quarrel from His pow'rful arm.
He needs no indirect or lawless course
To cut off those that have offended Him.
1. Mur. Who made thee then a bloody minister
When gallant-springing brave Plantagenet, 230
That princely novice, was struck dead by thee?
Clar. My brother's love, the Devil, and my rage.
1. Mur. Thy brother's love, our duty, and thy faults
Provoke us hither now to slaughter thee.
Clar. If you do love my brother, hate not me: 235
I am his brother, and I love him well.
If you are hired for meed, go back again,
And I will send you to my brother Gloucester,
Who shall reward you better for my life
Than Edward will for tidings of my death. 240
2. Mur. You are deceived. Your brother Gloucester hates you.
Clar. O, no, he loves me and he holds me dear:
Go you to him from me.
1. Mur. Ay, so we will. 245
Clar. Tell him, when that our princely father York
Blessed his three sons with his victorious arm
And charged us from his soul to love each other,
He little thought of this divided friendship:
Bid Gloucester think on this, and he will weep. 250
1. Mur. Ay, millstones, as he lessoned us to weep.
Clar. O do not slander him, for he is kind.
1. Mur. Right, as snow in harvest. Come, you deceive yourself;

272. **pent:** i.e., pent (shut) up.

'Tis he that sends us to destroy you here. 255
Clar. It cannot be, for he bewept my fortune,
And hugged me in his arms, and swore with sobs
That he would labor my delivery.
1. Mur. Why, so he doth, when he delivers you
From this earth's thralldom to the joys of heaven. 260
2. Mur. Make peace with God, for you must die, my lord.
Clar. Have you that holy feeling in your souls
To counsel me to make my peace with God,
And are you yet to your own souls so blind 265
That you will war with God by murd'ring me?
O sirs, consider, they that set you on
To do this deed will hate you for the deed.
2. Mur. What shall we do?
Clar. Relent, and save your souls. 270
Which of you, if you were a prince's son,
Being pent from liberty, as I am now,
If two such murderers as yourselves came to you,
Would not entreat for life?
1. Mur. Relent? No, 'tis cowardly and womanish. 275
Clar. Not to relent is beastly, savage, devilish.
[*To 2. Murderer*] My friend, I spy some pity in thy looks.
O, if thine eye be not a flatterer,
Come thou on my side, and entreat for me 280
As you would beg, were you in my distress.
A begging prince what beggar pities not?
2. Mur. Look behind you, my lord!
1. Mur. Take that! and that! (*Stabs him.*) If all this will not do, 285

289. **like Pilate:** Pilate washed his hands and refused to accept responsibility for the execution of Jesus. See Matt. 27:24.

Edward IV.
From an 1811 reprint of John Rastell, *The Pastime of People* (1529).

I'll drown you in the malmsey butt within.

Exit [with the body].

2. *Mur.* A bloody deed, and desperately dispatched!
How fain, like Pilate, would I wash my hands
Of this most grievous murder! 290

[Re-]enter *First Murderer.*

1. *Mur.* How now? What meanst thou that thou helpst me not?
By heaven, the Duke shall know how slack you have been.

2. *Mur.* I would he knew that I had saved his brother! 295
Take thou the fee and tell him what I say,
For I repent me that the Duke is slain. *Exit.*

1. *Mur.* So do not I. Go, coward as thou art.
Well, I'll go hide the body in some hole 300
Till that the Duke give order for his burial;
And when I have my meed, I will away,
For this will out, and then I must not stay.

Exit.

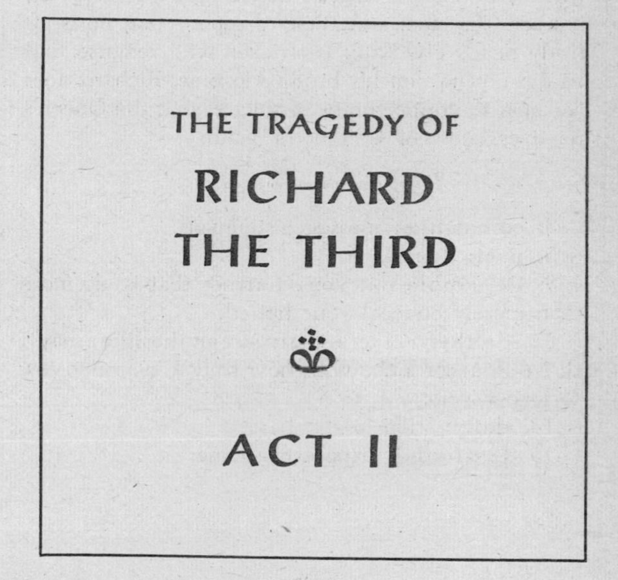
THE TRAGEDY OF
RICHARD
THE THIRD
ACT II

II. i. King Edward's persuasion results in peace between the Queen, Dorset, Rivers, Hastings, Buckingham, and Richard, all of whom swear to love each other. A chill is cast on the group, however, when the Queen urges the King to forgive his brother Clarence, and Richard reports that he is already dead. The King is stricken with remorse that he did not pardon his brother in time. Richard does not miss the opportunity to suggest that the Queen's relatives knew of Clarence's death.

---

3. **embassage:** message; summons.

5. **part:** depart.

8. **Dissemble not your hatred:** that is, do more than merely conceal your hatred.

12. **So thrive I as I truly swear the like:** may I thrive in accordance with how truly I keep my vow to love Rivers.

13. **dally:** trifle.

15. **Confound:** expose to shame.

ACT II

Scene I. [London. The Palace.]

Flourish. Enter the *King* [*Edward,*] sick, the *Queen, Lord Marquess Dorset,* [*Grey,*] *Rivers, Hastings, Catesby,* [and] *Buckingham.*

King. Why, so: now have I done a good day's work.
You peers, continue this united league.
I every day expect an embassage
From my Redeemer to redeem me hence;
And more in peace my soul shall part to heaven, 5
Since I have made my friends at peace on earth.
Hastings and Rivers, take each other's hand;
Dissemble not your hatred, swear your love.
Riv. By heaven, my soul is purged from grudging hate, 10
And with my hand I seal my true heart's love.
Hast. So thrive I as I truly swear the like!
King. Take heed you dally not before your king,
Lest He that is the supreme King of Kings
Confound your hidden falsehood, and award 15
Either of you to be the other's end.
Hast. So prosper I as I swear perfect love!
Riv. And I as I love Hastings with my heart!
King. Madam, yourself is not exempt from this;
Nor you, son Dorset; Buckingham, nor you: 20
You have been factious one against the other.

23. **unfeignedly:** without pretense; sincerely.

46. **cordial:** restorative.

49. **period:** conclusion; i.e., to complete it; see I. iii. 273.

Anthony Woodville, Earl Rivers.
From a costume design by J. R. Planché (1829).

Wife, love Lord Hastings, let him kiss your hand,
And what you do, do it unfeignedly.
Queen. There, Hastings. I will never more remember
Our former hatred, so thrive I and mine! 25
King. Dorset, embrace him; Hastings, love Lord Marquess.
Dor. This interchange of love, I here protest,
Upon my part shall be inviolable. 30
Hast. And so swear I. [*They embrace.*]
King. Now, princely Buckingham, seal thou this league
With thy embracements to my wife's allies,
And make me happy in your unity. 35
Buck. [*To the Queen*] Whenever Buckingham doth turn his hate
Upon your Grace, but with all duteous love
Doth cherish you and yours, God punish me
With hate in those where I expect most love! 40
When I have most need to employ a friend,
And most assured that he is a friend,
Deep, hollow, treacherous, and full of guile
Be he unto me! This do I beg of heaven,
When I am cold in love to you or yours. *Embrace.* 45
King. A pleasing cordial, princely Buckingham,
Is this thy vow unto my sickly heart.
There wanteth now our brother Gloucester here,
To make the blessed period of this peace.
Buck. And in good time, 50
Here comes Sir Richard Ratcliffe and the Duke.

58. **swelling:** puffed up with pride.

61. **intelligence:** information.

64. **hardly borne:** deeply resented.

71. **cousin Buckingham:** Buckingham's grandmother was Anne Neville, sister to Richard's mother, Cicely Neville.

74. **all without desert:** without my having deserved it at all.

Enter *Ratcliffe* and [*Richard, Duke of*] *Gloucester.*

Rich. Good morrow to my sovereign king and queen;
And, princely peers, a happy time of day!
King. Happy indeed, as we have spent the day: 55
Gloucester, we have done deeds of charity,
Made peace of enmity, fair love of hate,
Between these swelling wrong-incensed peers.
Rich. A blessed labor, my most sovereign lord.
Among this princely heap, if any here 60
By false intelligence or wrong surmise
Hold me a foe;
If I unwittingly, or in my rage,
Have aught committed that is hardly borne
By any in this presence, I desire 65
To reconcile me to his friendly peace.
'Tis death to me to be at enmity:
I hate it, and desire all good men's love.
First, madam, I entreat true peace of you,
Which I will purchase with my duteous service; 70
Of you, my noble cousin Buckingham,
If ever any grudge were lodged between us;
Of you, and you, Lord Rivers, and of Dorset,
That, all without desert, have frowned on me;
Dukes, earls, lords, gentlemen—indeed, of all. 75
I do not know that Englishman alive
With whom my soul is any jot at odds
More than the infant that is born tonight.
I thank my God for my humility.
Queen. A holy day shall this be kept hereafter: 80

81. **compounded:** made up; agreed.

83. **take . . . to your grace:** i.e., pardon.

85. **flouted:** mocked.

95. **Mercury:** the messenger of the gods and the personification of speed.

97. **lag:** late.

99. **Nearer in bloody thoughts, but not in blood:** a hint that the Queen's faction is responsible for Clarence's death. **Blood** means "kinship."

101. **current:** free; i.e., pass freely without suspicion that their loyalty is counterfeit; see I. ii. 89 and I. iii. 297.

106. **forfeit . . . of my servant's life:** i.e., he asks that his servant's life be spared despite the fact that he slew a man.

I would to God all strifes were well compounded.
My sovereign lord, I do beseech your Highness
To take our brother Clarence to your grace.
Rich. Why, madam, have I off'red love for this,
To be so flouted in this royal presence? 85
Who knows not that the gentle Duke is dead?
They all start.
You do him injury to scorn his corse.
King. Who knows not he is dead? Who knows he is?
Queen. All-seeing heaven, what a world is this!
Buck. Look I so pale, Lord Dorset, as the rest? 90
Dor. Ay, my good lord; and no man in the presence
But his red color hath forsook his cheeks.
King. Is Clarence dead? The order was reversed.
Rich. But he, poor man, by your first order died,
And that a winged Mercury did bear: 95
Some tardy cripple bare the countermand,
That came too lag to see him buried.
God grant that some, less noble and less loyal,
Nearer in bloody thoughts, but not in blood,
Deserve not worse than wretched Clarence did, 100
And yet go current from suspicion!

Enter [*Lord Stanley,*] *Earl of Derby.*

Der. A boon, my sovereign, for my service done!
[*Kneeling.*]
King. I prithee peace. My soul is full of sorrow.
Der. I will not rise unless your Highness hear me.
King. Then say at once what is it thou requests. 105
Der. The forfeit, sovereign, of my servant's life,

114. **be advised:** think it over.

119. **Oxford had me down:** this incident is not recorded and is probably another touch to make Clarence a sympathetic character and Richard's assassination of him a blacker deed.

131. **straight:** immediately.

Who slew today a riotous gentleman
Lately attendant on the Duke of Norfolk.
King. Have I a tongue to doom my brother's death,
And shall that tongue give pardon to a slave? 110
My brother killed no man—his fault was thought—
And yet his punishment was bitter death.
Who sued to me for him? Who, in my wrath,
Kneeled at my feet and bid me be advised?
Who spoke of brotherhood? Who spoke of love? 115
Who told me how the poor soul did forsake
The mighty Warwick and did fight for me?
Who told me, in the field at Tewkesbury,
When Oxford had me down, he rescued me
And said, "Dear brother, live, and be a king"? 120
Who told me, when we both lay in the field
Frozen almost to death, how he did lap me
Even in his garments, and did give himself,
All thin and naked, to the numb-cold night?
All this from my remembrance brutish wrath 125
Sinfully plucked, and not a man of you
Had so much grace to put it in my mind.
But when your carters or your waiting vassals
Have done a drunken slaughter and defaced
The precious image of our dear Redeemer, 130
You straight are on your knees for pardon, pardon;
And I, unjustly too, must grant it you. [*Derby rises.*]
But for my brother not a man would speak,
Nor I, ungracious, speak unto myself
For him, poor soul! The proudest of you all 135
Have been beholding to him in his life;
Yet none of you would once beg for his life.

140. **closet:** chamber.
145. **still:** continually.
148. **wait upon:** attend.

II. ii. The Duchess of York, mother of King Edward, Clarence, and Richard, mourns Clarence's death. She is joined by Queen Elizabeth, lamenting the death of her husband. Richard, Buckingham, and some of their associates appear and counsel comfort, and Buckingham points out that steps should be taken to bring Prince Edward from Ludlow to be crowned King. It is agreed that a small escort would be desirable for fear of provoking new outbreaks of hostility against Yorkist supremacy in the kingdom. Secretly Buckingham and Richard plot to separate the young Prince from the Queen and her kin.

---

9. **cousins:** a term loosely used for relations not of the nearest degree; the children are the Duchess' grandchildren.
12. **were:** would be.

O God! I fear Thy justice will take hold
On me and you, and mine and yours, for this.
Come, Hastings, help me to my closet. Ah, poor 140
Clarence! *Exeunt some with King and Queen.*

Rich. This is the fruits of rashness! Marked you not
How that the guilty kindred of the Queen
Looked pale when they did hear of Clarence' death?
O, they did urge it still unto the King! 145
God will revenge it. Come, lords, will you go
To comfort Edward with our company?

Buck. We wait upon your Grace.

Exeunt.

Scene II. [London. The Palace.]

Enter the *Old Duchess of York,* with the *Two Children* of *Clarence* [*Edward* and *Margaret Plantagenet*].

Boy. Good grandam, tell us, is our father dead?

Duch. No, boy.

Girl. Why do you weep so oft, and beat your breast,
And cry "O Clarence, my unhappy son"? 5

Boy. Why do you look on us, and shake your head,
And call us orphans, wretches, castaways,
If that our noble father were alive?

Duch. My pretty cousins, you mistake me both.
I do lament the sickness of the King, 10
As loath to lose him, not your father's death:
It were lost sorrow to wail one that's lost.

20. **Incapable and shallow:** incapable of understanding such profound matters.

25. **impeachments:** accusations.

32. **visor:** mask.

A widow in mourning habit.
From a costume design by J. R. Planché (1829).

Boy. Then you conclude, my grandam, he is dead.
The King mine uncle is to blame for it:
God will revenge it, whom I will importune 15
With earnest prayers all to that effect.
Girl. And so will I.
Duch. Peace, children, peace! The King doth love you well.
Incapable and shallow innocents, 20
You cannot guess who caused your father's death.
Boy. Grandam, we can; for my good uncle Gloucester
Told me the King, provoked to it by the Queen,
Devised impeachments to imprison him; 25
And when my uncle told me so, he wept,
And pitied me, and kindly kissed my cheek;
Bade me rely on him as on my father,
And he would love me dearly as a child.
Duch. Ah, that deceit should steal such gentle shape 30
And with a virtuous visor hide deep vice!
He is my son—ay, and therein my shame;
Yet from my dugs he drew not this deceit.
Boy. Think you my uncle did dissemble, grandam? 35
Duch. Ay, boy.
Boy. I cannot think it. Hark! What noise is this?

Enter the *Queen* [*Elizabeth,*] with her hair about her ears, *Rivers* and *Dorset* after her.

Queen. Ah, who shall hinder me to wail and weep,
To chide my fortune, and torment myself?

46. **want:** lack; see I. i. 16.

55. **two mirrors of his princely semblance:** i.e., two children who resemble him.

65. **overgo:** go beyond; surpass.

69. **dolor:** sorrow.

I'll join with black despair against my soul, 40
And to myself become an enemy.

Duch. What means this scene of rude impatience?

Queen. To make an act of tragic violence.
Edward, my lord, thy son, our king, is dead!
Why grow the branches when the root is gone? 45
Why wither not the leaves that want their sap?
If you will live, lament; if die, be brief,
That our swift-winged souls may catch the King's,
Or like obedient subjects follow him
To his new kingdom of ne'er-changing night. 50

Duch. Ah, so much interest have I in thy sorrow
As I had title in thy noble husband.
I have bewept a worthy husband's death,
And lived with looking on his images;
But now two mirrors of his princely semblance 55
Are cracked in pieces by malignant death,
And I for comfort have but one false glass,
That grieves me when I see my shame in him.
Thou art a widow; yet thou art a mother,
And hast the comfort of thy children left; 60
But death hath snatched my husband from mine arms
And plucked two crutches from my feeble hands,
Clarence and Edward. O, what cause have I,
Thine being but a moiety of my moan,
To overgo thy woes and drown thy cries! 65

Boy. Ah, aunt! you wept not for our father's death.
How can we aid you with our kindred tears?

Girl. Our fatherless distress was left unmoaned:
Your widow-dolor likewise be unwept!

Queen. Give me no help in lamentation; 70

72. **reduce:** bring.

73. **the watery moon:** so called because it controlled tides and was believed to cause rain.

79. **stay:** support; comfort.

85. **dear:** grievous; extreme.

89. **parceled:** parceled out among them; they each weep for only one loss.

I am not barren to bring forth complaints.
All springs reduce their currents to mine eyes,
That I, being governed by the watery moon,
May send forth plenteous tears to drown the world.
Ah for my husband, for my dear lord Edward! 75

Child. Ah for our father, for our dear lord Clarence!

Duch. Alas for both, both mine, Edward and Clarence!

Queen. What stay had I but Edward? and he's gone. 80

Child. What stay had we but Clarence? and he's gone.

Duch. What stays had I but they? and they are gone.

Queen. Was never widow had so dear a loss. 85

Child. Were never orphans had so dear a loss.

Duch. Was never mother had so dear a loss.
Alas! I am the mother of these griefs:
Their woes are parceled, mine is general.
She for an Edward weeps, and so do I; 90
I for a Clarence weep, so doth not she:
These babes for Clarence weep, and so do I;
I for an Edward weep, so do not they.
Alas, you three on me, threefold distressed,
Pour all your tears! I am your sorrow's nurse, 95
And I will pamper it with lamentation.

Dor. Comfort, dear mother; God is much displeased
That you take with unthankfulness His doing.
In common worldly things 'tis called ungrateful 100
With dull unwillingness to repay a debt

123. **cloudy:** clouded with grief.

Edward V.
From an 1811 reprint of John Rastell, *The Pastime of People* (1529).

Which with a bounteous hand was kindly lent;
Much more to be thus opposite with heaven
For it requires the royal debt it lent you.
Riv. Madam, bethink you like a careful mother 105
Of the young Prince your son. Send straight for him;
Let him be crowned; in him your comfort lives.
Drown desperate sorrow in dead Edward's grave,
And plant your joys in living Edward's throne.

Enter *Richard, Buckingham,* [*Stanley, Earl of*] *Derby, Hastings,* and *Ratcliffe.*

Rich. Sister, have comfort. All of us have cause 110
To wail the dimming of our shining star;
But none can help our harms by wailing them.
Madam, my mother, I do cry you mercy;
I did not see your Grace. Humbly on my knee
I crave your blessing. 115
Duch. God bless thee, and put meekness in thy breast,
Love, charity, obedience, and true duty!
Rich. Amen!—[*Aside*] and make me die a good old man! 120
That is the butt end of a mother's blessing;
I marvel that her Grace did leave it out.
Buck. You cloudy princes and heart-sorrowing peers
That bear this heavy mutual load of moan, 125
Now cheer each other in each other's love.
Though we have spent our harvest of this king,
We are to reap the harvest of his son.

129-30. **The broken rancor of your high-swol'n hates,/ But lately splintered, knit, and joined together:** their mutual hatred is compared to an infection or boil, swollen with pus to the breaking point and then healed.

132. **Meseemeth good:** i.e., it seems a good idea to me.

133. **fet:** fetched.

140. **the estate is green and yet ungoverned:** the Prince's reign is so new that his officials have not yet had a chance to set up the machinery of government.

150. **haply:** perhaps.

152. **meet:** suitable.

155. **post:** ride with all speed; see I. i. 158.

157. **censures:** judgments.

The broken rancor of your high-swol'n hates,
But lately splintered, knit, and joined together, 130
Must gently be preserved, cherished, and kept.
Meseemeth good that, with some little train,
Forthwith from Ludlow the young Prince be fet
Hither to London, to be crowned our king.

Riv. Why with some little train, my Lord of Buckingham? 135

Buck. Marry, my lord, lest by a multitude
The new-healed wound of malice should break out,
Which would be so much the more dangerous
By how much the estate is green and yet ungoverned. 140
Where every horse bears his commanding rein
And may direct his course as please himself,
As well the fear of harm as harm apparent,
In my opinion, ought to be prevented.

Rich. I hope the King made peace with all of us; 145
And the compact is firm and true in me.

Riv. And so in me; and so, I think, in all.
Yet, since it is but green, it should be put
To no apparent likelihood of breach,
Which haply by much company might be urged. 150
Therefore I say with noble Buckingham
That it is meet so few should fetch the Prince.

Hast. And so say I.

Rich. Then be it so; and go we to determine
Who they shall be that straight shall post to Ludlow. 155
Madam, and you, my sister, will you go
To give your censures in this business?

Both. With all our hearts.

Exeunt. Manent Buckingham and Richard.

161. **sort occasion:** select opportunity.

162. **index:** prologue.

164. **consistory:** meeting place; i.e., the place where I turn for counsel.

II. iii. Three citizens of London present the general feeling of the city at news of the King's death. All fear civil discord in view of the Prince's youth and the necessity of his guidance by more mature advisers. It is clear that neither the Duke of Gloucester nor the Prince's maternal uncles are trusted.

6-7. **seldom comes the better:** a proverbial expression of pessimism. The citizen doubts that the state of the realm will be as sound as before.

8. **giddy:** disordered; unsettled.

Buck. My lord, whoever journeys to the Prince,
For God's sake let not us two stay at home; 160
For by the way I'll sort occasion,
As index to the story we late talked of,
To part the Queen's proud kindred from the Prince.
Rich. My other self, my counsel's consistory,
My oracle, my prophet, my dear cousin, 165
I, as a child, will go by thy direction.
Toward Ludlow then, for we'll not stay behind.
Exeunt.

Scene III. [London. A street.]

Enter one *Citizen* at one door and another at the other.

1. Cit. Good morrow, neighbor. Whither away so fast?
2. Cit. I promise you, I scarcely know myself.
Hear you the news abroad?
1. Cit. Yes, that the King is dead. 5
2. Cit. Ill news, by'r Lady—seldom comes the better:
I fear, I fear, 'twill prove a giddy world.

Enter another *Citizen.*

3. Cit. Neighbors, God speed!
1. Cit. Give you good morrow, sir. 10
3. Cit. Doth the news hold of good King Edward's death?

13. **the while:** our times and those who live in them.

17. **Woe to that land that's governed by a child:** another proverbial idea from the Bible; see Eccles. 10:16.

19. **in his nonage:** while he is a minor.

25. **wot:** knows.

27. **politic:** shrewd.

33. **emulation:** envy.

36. **haught:** haughty.

38. **solace:** be cheerful.

2. *Cit.* Ay, sir, it is too true. God help the while!
3. *Cit.* Then, masters, look to see a troublous world.
1. *Cit.* No, no! By God's good grace his son shall reign. 15
3. *Cit.* Woe to that land that's governed by a child!
2. *Cit.* In him there is a hope of government,
Which, in his nonage, council under him,
And, in his full and ripened years, himself, 20
No doubt shall then, and till then, govern well.
1. *Cit.* So stood the state when Henry the Sixth
Was crowned in Paris but at nine months old.
3. *Cit.* Stood the state so? No, no, good friends, God wot! 25
For then this land was famously enriched
With politic grave counsel; then the King
Had virtuous uncles to protect his Grace.
1. *Cit.* Why, so hath this, both by his father and mother. 30
3. *Cit.* Better it were they all came by his father,
Or by his father there were none at all;
For emulation who shall now be nearest
Will touch us all too near, if God prevent not.
O, full of danger is the Duke of Gloucester! 35
And the Queen's sons and brothers haught and proud;
And were they to be ruled, and not to rule,
This sickly land might solace as before.
1. *Cit.* Come, come, we fear the worst. All will be well. 40
3. *Cit.* When clouds are seen, wise men put on their cloaks;

46. **sort:** arrange.

49. **reason:** talk; see I. iv. 163.

51. **Before the days of change, still is it so:** that is, it is always so when change is threatened.

II. iv. Queen Elizabeth, her mother-in-law, the Duchess of York, and the Archbishop of York are enjoying the childish talk of the Queen's second son, the Duke of York, when they receive word that the Prince of Wales has been seized by Richard, and his escorts, Rivers, Grey, and Vaughan, have been imprisoned at Pomfret. The Queen decides at once to seek sanctuary for herself and the young Duke of York, and the Archbishop promises to give her the Great Seal of the realm and do all he can for her interests.

When great leaves fall, then winter is at hand;
When the sun sets, who doth not look for night?
Untimely storms makes men expcct a dearth. 45
All may be well; but if God sort it so,
'Tis more than we deserve or I expect.

2. *Cit.* Truly, the hearts of men are full of fear:
You cannot reason, almost, with a man
That looks not heavily and full of dread. 50

3. *Cit.* Before the days of change, still is it so.
By a divine instinct men's minds mistrust
Ensuing danger; as, by proof, we see
The water swell before a boist'rous storm.
But leave it all to God. Whither away? 55

2. *Cit.* Marry, we were sent for to the justices.

3. *Cit.* And so was I. I'll bear you company.

Exeunt.

Scene IV. [London. The Palace.]

Enter [the] *Archbishop* [*of York*], [the] young [*Duke of*] *York*, the *Queen* [*Elizabeth*], and the *Duchess* [*of York*].

Arch. Last night, I hear, they lay at Stony Stratford;
And at Northampton they do rest tonight;
Tomorrow, or next day, they will be here.

Duch. I long with all my heart to see the Prince: 5
I hope he is much grown since last I saw him.

15. **grace:** virtue; healing power.

23. **gracious:** full of grace.

26. **troth:** faith; **rememb'red:** reminded.

27. **given my uncle's Grace a flout:** had a laugh at my uncle's expense.

31-2. **they say my uncle grew so fast/ That he could gnaw a crust at two hours old:** the tradition that Richard was born with teeth derives originally from John Rous, *Historia regum Angliae* (c. 1490).

Queen. But I hear no. They say my son of York
Has almost overta'en him in his growth.
York. Ay, mother; but I would not have it so.
Duch. Why, my good cousin? it is good to grow. 10
York. Grandam, one night as we did sit at supper,
My uncle Rivers talked how I did grow
More than my brother. "Ay," quoth my uncle Gloucester,
"Small herbs have grace; great weeds do grow apace." 15
And since, methinks, I would not grow so fast,
Because sweet flow'rs are slow and weeds make haste.
Duch. Good faith, good faith, the saying did not hold
In him that did object the same to thee: 20
He was the wretched'st thing when he was young,
So long a-growing and so leisurely
That, if his rule were true, he should be gracious.
Arch. And so no doubt he is, my gracious madam.
Duch. I hope he is; but yet let mothers doubt. 25
York. Now, by my troth, if I had been rememb'red,
I could have given my uncle's Grace a flout,
To touch his growth nearer than he touched mine.
Duch. How, my young York? I prithee let me hear it. 30
York. Marry, they say my uncle grew so fast
That he could gnaw a crust at two hours old:
'Twas full two years ere I could get a tooth.
Grandam, this would have been a biting jest.
Duch. I prithee, pretty York, who told thee this? 35
York. Grandam, his nurse.

40. **parlous:** perilous; clever; **Go to:** that's enough; **shrewd:** sharp.

42. **Pitchers have ears:** the proverbial expression "Little pitchers have big ears," meaning that children hear more than one expects.

60. **jut:** loom threateningly.

61. **aweless:** without awe; i.e., lacking the awful majesty which should repel usurpers.

63. **as in a map:** as though the whole course of future events were mapped out for me.

Duch. His nurse? Why, she was dead ere thou wast born.
York. If 'twere not she, I cannot tell who told me.
Queen. A parlous boy! Go to, you are too shrewd. 40
Duch. Good madam, be not angry with the child.
Queen. Pitchers have ears.

Enter a *Messenger.*

Arch. Here comes a messenger. What news?
Mess. Such news, my lord, as grieves me to report.
Queen. How doth the Prince? 45
Mess. Well, madam, and in health.
Duch. What is thy news?
Mess. Lord Rivers and Lord Grey are sent to Pomfret,
And with them Sir Thomas Vaughan, prisoners. 50
Duch. Who hath committed them?
Mess. The mighty Dukes,
Gloucester and Buckingham.
Arch. For what offense?
Mess. The sum of all I can I have disclosed. 55
Why or for what the nobles were committed
Is all unknown to me, my gracious lord.
Queen. Ay me! I see the ruin of my house.
The tiger now hath seized the gentle hind;
Insulting tyranny begins to jut 60
Upon the innocent and aweless throne.
Welcome destruction, blood, and massacre!
I see, as in a map, the end of all.

72. **preposterous:** monstrously unnatural.

73. **spleen:** angry fit.

75. **sanctuary:** under the laws of the medieval church, a fugitive from justice or a debtor was immune from arrest when he took refuge in a church or some other sacred place. In similar fashion, the Queen expects to be safe from violence under the protection of the church.

82-3. **The seal I keep:** the Great Seal of England, a symbol of the power of the crown; **so betide to me/ As well I tender you and all of yours:** may what happens to me accord with how I take care of you and yours.

Duch. Accursed and unquiet wrangling days,
How many of you have mine eyes beheld! 65
My husband lost his life to get the crown,
And often up and down my sons were tossed
For me to joy and weep their gain and loss;
And being seated, and domestic broils
Clean overblown, themselves, the conquerors, 70
Make war upon themselves, brother to brother,
Blood to blood, self against self. O preposterous
And frantic outrage, end thy damned spleen,
Or let me die, to look on earth no more!

Queen. Come, come, my boy; we will to sanctuary. 75
Madam, farewell.

Duch. Stay, I will go with you.

Queen. You have no cause.

Arch. [*To the Queen*] My gracious lady, go,
And thither bear your treasure and your goods. 80
For my part, I'll resign unto your Grace
The seal I keep; and so betide to me
As well I tender you and all of yours!
Go, I'll conduct you to the sanctuary.

Exeunt.

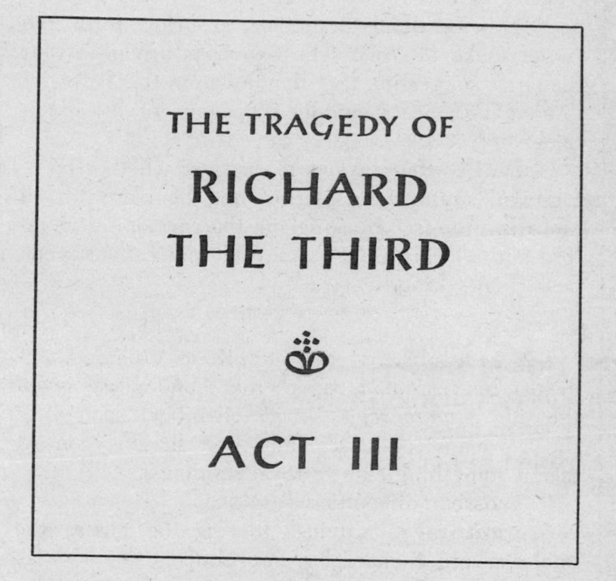

THE TRAGEDY OF

RICHARD THE THIRD

ACT III

III. i. Richard and Buckingham arrive in London with the Prince of Wales. The lad is distressed to find that his mother and brother are not on hand to greet him, and Lord Hastings informs them that the Queen has fled to sanctuary with her son. Richard persuades Cardinal Bourchier to bring forth the young Duke of York. The two boys are uneasy at Richard's suggestion that they lodge in the Tower of London and are generally suspicious of his intentions.

Richard is now anxious to discover whether Hastings will support his plot; if not, he plans to kill him. He promises Buckingham the earldom of Hereford and all Edward IV's movable possessions when he becomes king.

1-2. **London . . . your chamber:** William Camden, in his *Britannia,* reports that London was given the title *camera regis* (king's chamber) soon after the Norman conquest. **Chamber** in this context means something akin to royal residence.

6. **crosses:** difficulties.

8. **want more uncles:** that is, he misses the uncles whom Richard has imprisoned.

14. **jumpeth:** agrees.

ACT III

Scene I. [London. A street.]

The trumpets sound. Enter young *Prince* [*Edward of Wales*], the *Dukes of Gloucester* and *Buckingham*, *Lord Cardinal* [*Bourchier, Catesby*], with others.

Buck. Welcome, sweet Prince, to London, to your chamber.
Rich. Welcome, dear cousin, my thoughts' sovereign:
The weary way hath made you melancholy. 5
Prince. No, uncle; but our crosses on the way
Have made it tedious, wearisome, and heavy.
I want more uncles here to welcome me.
Rich. Sweet Prince, the untainted virtue of your years 10
Hath not yet dived into the world's deceit:
Nor more can you distinguish of a man
Than of his outward show, which, God He knows,
Seldom or never jumpeth with the heart.
Those uncles which you want were dangerous; 15
Your Grace attended to their sug'red words
But looked not on the poison of their hearts:
God keep you from them, and from such false friends!
Prince. God keep me from false friends!—but they were none. 20

29. **slug:** sluggard.
35. **On what occasion:** i.e., why.
40. **peevish:** perverse.
43. **presently:** at once.
45. **jealous:** suspicious.

Rich. My lord, the Mayor of London comes to greet you.

Enter *Lord Mayor* [and his *Train*].

May. God bless your Grace with health and happy days!

Prince. I thank you, good my lord, and thank you all. 25

[*Exeunt Mayor and his Train.*]

I thought my mother and my brother York
Would long ere this have met us on the way.
Fie, what a slug is Hastings, that he comes not
To tell us whether they will come or no! 30

Enter *Lord Hastings.*

Buck. And, in good time, here comes the sweating lord.

Prince. Welcome, my lord. What, will our mother come?

Hast. On what occasion God He knows, not I, 35
The Queen your mother and your brother York
Have taken sanctuary. The tender Prince
Would fain have come with me to meet your Grace,
But by his mother was perforce withheld.

Buck. Fie, what an indirect and peevish course 40
Is this of hers! Lord Cardinal, will your Grace
Persuade the Queen to send the Duke of York
Unto his princely brother presently?
If she deny, Lord Hastings, go with him
And from her jealous arms pluck him perforce. 45

53. **senseless-obstinate:** obstinate against all reason.

54. **ceremonious:** observant of formalities.

58. **deserved the place:** i.e., who have committed some crime for which they would be punished were they not protected by sanctuary.

59. **have the wit to claim the place:** are possessed of mature judgment to make their own decision to claim sanctuary. The young Duke, on the other hand, has been forced into sanctuary by his mother.

75. **the Tower:** the Tower of London contained royal apartments and was the residence of more than one sovereign, including Edward IV before his coronation. It did not really acquire connotations of danger until a later age.

Card. My Lord of Buckingham, if my weak oratory
Can from his mother win the Duke of York,
Anon expect him here; but if she be obdurate
To mild entreaties, God in heaven forbid
We should infringe the holy privilege 50
Of blessed sanctuary! Not for all this land
Would I be guilty of so great a sin.

Buck. You are too senseless-obstinate, my lord,
Too ceremonious and traditional.
Weigh it but with the grossness of this age, 55
You break not sanctuary in seizing him:
The benefit thereof is always granted
To those whose dealings have deserved the place
And those who have the wit to claim the place.
This prince hath neither claimed it nor deserved it, 60
And therefore, in mine opinion, cannot have it.
Then, taking him from thence that is not there,
You break no privilege nor charter there.
Oft have I heard of sanctuary men,
But sanctuary children ne'er till now. 65

Card. My lord, you shall o'errule my mind for once.
Come on, Lord Hastings, will you go with me?

Hast. I go, my lord.

Prince. Good lords, make all the speedy haste you
may. 70

Exeunt Cardinal and Hastings.

Say, uncle Gloucester, if our brother come,
Where shall we sojourn till our coronation?

Rich. Where it seems best unto your royal self.
If I may counsel you, some day or two
Your Highness shall repose you at the Tower; 75

78. **of any place:** that is, of all places it appeals to me least.

79. **Julius Cæsar:** although not recorded earlier, English chroniclers established a tradition that Julius Cæsar was responsible for building the Tower.

81. **re-edified:** rebuilt.

88. **general all-ending day:** i.e., Day of Judgment.

92. **characters:** writings; i.e., historical records.

93-4. **like the formal Vice, Iniquity,/ I moralize two meanings in one word:** Richard presumes that the Prince heard his last sentence only faintly, and for his benefit makes a statement that ends in the same words without containing the same threat. **Vice** was a traditional figure in morality plays.

102. **An if:** if.

105-6. **Short summers lightly have a forward spring:** a rephrasing of the proverb expressed in ll. 89-90. **Lightly** means usually or commonly.

Then where you please, and shall be thought most fit
For your best health and recreation.

Prince. I do not like the Tower, of any place.
Did Julius Cæsar build that place, my lord?

Buck. He did, my gracious lord, begin that place, 80
Which, since, succeeding ages have re-edified.

Prince. Is it upon record, or else reported
Successively from age to age, he built it?

Buck. Upon record, my gracious lord.

Prince. But say, my lord, it were not regist'red, 85
Methinks the truth should live from age to age,
As 'twere retailed to all posterity,
Even to the general all-ending day.

Rich. [*Aside*] So wise so young, they say, do never live long. 90

Prince. What say you, uncle?

Rich. I say, without characters fame lives long.
[*Aside*] Thus, like the formal Vice, Iniquity,
I moralize two meanings in one word.

Prince. That Julius Cæsar was a famous man: 95
With what his valor did enrich his wit,
His wit set down to make his valor live.
Death makes no conquest of this conqueror,
For now he lives in fame, though not in life.
I'll tell you what, my cousin Buckingham— 100

Buck. What, my gracious lord?

Prince. An if I live until I be a man,
I'll win our ancient right in France again,
Or die a soldier as I lived a king.

Rich. [*Aside*] Short summers lightly have a forward spring. 105

109. **our:** the royal plural.

113. **late:** lately.

126. **With all my heart:** Richard's apparent kindness is really irony.

129. **toy:** a thing of little value.

Enter [the] young [*Duke of*] *York, Hastings,*
and *Cardinal* [*Bourchier*].

Buck. Now, in good time, here comes the Duke of York.

Prince. Richard of York, how fares our noble brother? 110

York. Well, my dread lord—so must I call you now.

Prince. Ay, brother, to our grief, as it is yours:
Too late he died that might have kept that title,
Which by his death hath lost much majesty.

Rich. How fares our cousin, noble Lord of York? 115

York. I thank you, gentle uncle. O my lord,
You said that idle weeds are fast in growth:
The Prince my brother hath outgrown me far.

Rich. He hath, my lord.

York. And therefore is he idle? 120

Rich. O my fair cousin, I must not say so.

York. Then he is more beholding to you than I.

Rich. He may command me as my sovereign,
But you have power in me as in a kinsman.

York. I pray you, uncle, give me this dagger. 125

Rich. My dagger, little cousin? With all my heart.

Prince. A beggar, brother?

York. Of my kind uncle, that I know will give,
And being but a toy, which is no grief to give.

Rich. A greater gift than that I'll give my cousin. 130

York. A greater gift? O, that's the sword to it.

Rich. Ay, gentle cousin, were it light enough.

133. **light:** slight.

137. **weigh:** value.

144. **will still be cross in talk:** that is, is always a quibbler, given to punning.

148-49. **Because that I am little, like an ape,/ He thinks that you should bear me on your shoulders: me** is emphatic; that is, "**me** instead of the hump you bear."

150-51. **sharp-provided:** quick and pointed.

York. O, then I see you will part but with light gifts!
In weightier things you'll say a beggar nay. 135
Rich. It is too heavy for your Grace to wear.
York. I weigh it lightly, were it heavier.
Rich. What, would you have my weapon, little lord?
York. I would, that I might thank you as you call me. 140
Rich. How?
York. Little.
Prince. My Lord of York will still be cross in talk.
Uncle, your Grace knows how to bear with him. 145
York. You mean, to bear me, not to bear with me.
Uncle, my brother mocks both you and me:
Because that I am little, like an ape,
He thinks that you should bear me on your shoulders.
Buck. [*Aside to Hastings*] With what a sharp-provided wit he reasons! 150
To mitigate the scorn he gives his uncle,
He prettily and aptly taunts himself:
So cunning, and so young, is wonderful.
Rich. My lord, will't please you pass along? 155
Myself and my good cousin Buckingham
Will to your mother, to entreat of her
To meet you at the Tower and welcome you.
York. What, will you go unto the Tower, my lord?
Prince. My Lord Protector needs will have it so. 160
York. I shall not sleep in quiet at the Tower.
Rich. Why, what should you fear?

173. **perilous:** clever; see II. iv. 40.

174. **capable:** of good understanding; see **incapable,** II. ii. 20.

176. **let them rest:** enough talk of them.

York. Marry, my uncle Clarence' angry ghost:
My grandam told me he was murdered there.
Prince. I fear no uncles dead. 165
Rich. Nor none that live, I hope.
Prince. An if they live, I hope I need not fear.
But come, my lord; and with a heavy heart,
Thinking on them, go I unto the Tower.
A sennet. Exeunt Prince [Edward], York, Hastings, [Cardinal Bourchier, and others]. Manent Richard, Buckingham, and Catesby.
Buck. Think you, my lord, this little prating York 170
Was not incensed by his subtle mother
To taunt and scorn you thus opprobriously?
Rich. No doubt, no doubt. O, 'tis a perilous boy,
Bold, quick, ingenious, forward, capable:
He is all the mother's, from the top to toe. 175
Buck. Well, let them rest. Come hither, Catesby.
Thou art sworn as deeply to effect what we intend
As closely to conceal what we impart.
Thou knowest our reasons urged upon the way.
What thinkst thou? Is it not an easy matter 180
To make William Lord Hastings of our mind
For the installment of this noble Duke
In the seat royal of this famous isle?
Cates. He for his father's sake so loves the Prince
That he will not be won to aught against him. 185
Buck. What thinkst thou then of Stanley? Will not he?
Cates. He will do all in all as Hastings doth.
Buck. Well then, no more but this: go, gentle Catesby, 190

191. **as it were far off, sound:** casually or indirectly test.

192. **How he doth stand affected to our purpose:** i.e., what attitude he will take toward our seizure of the throne.

194. **sit:** confer.

200. **divided councils:** a council of the chief officials of the realm was to plan the coronation of Prince Edward; Richard also intends to hold a private council to plan his own coronation.

218. **complots:** conspiracies.

219-20. **Something we will determine:** we'll think of something by way of excuse.

And, as it were far off, sound thou Lord Hastings
How he doth stand affected to our purpose,
And summon him tomorrow to the Tower
To sit about the coronation.
If thou dost find him tractable to us, 195
Encourage him, and tell him all our reasons:
If he be leaden, icy, cold, unwilling,
Be thou so too, and so break off the talk,
And give us notice of his inclination;
For we tomorrow hold divided councils, 200
Wherein thyself shalt highly be employed.

Rich. Commend me to Lord William. Tell him, Catesby,
His ancient knot of dangerous adversaries
Tomorrow are let blood at Pomfret Castle, 205
And bid my lord, for joy of this good news,
Give Mistress Shore one gentle kiss the more.

Buck. Good Catesby, go effect this business soundly.

Cates. My good lords both, with all the heed I can. 210

Rich. Shall we hear from you, Catesby, ere we sleep?

Cates. You shall, my lord.

Rich. At Crosby House, there shall you find us both. 215

Exit Catesby.

Buck. Now, my lord, what shall we do if we perceive
Lord Hastings will not yield to our complots?

Rich. Chop off his head! Something we will determine. 220

226. **betimes:** early.

227. **digest our complots in some form:** outline the details of our conspiracy in orderly fashion.

III. ii. Hastings is warned by Stanley of Richard's plot, but despite this and a visit by Catesby, who performs his mission to sound the Lord Chamberlain about crowning Richard instead of the Prince, he affirms his allegiance to the son of Edward IV and is optimistic about the future. As he sets out for a council meeting at the Tower, Buckingham meets him and hints obliquely at Richard's intention that he shall not leave the Tower alive.

---

9. **commends him:** offers his dutiful respects.

12. **the boar:** i.e., Richard. The reference is to the **boar** symbol which he used; **rased off his helm:** literally, knocked off his helmet; figuratively, cut off his head.

And look when I am King, claim thou of me
The earldom of Hereford and all the movables
Whereof the King my brother was possessed.
Buck. I'll claim that promise at your Grace's hand.
Rich. And look to have it yielded with all kindness. 225
Come, let us sup betimes, that afterwards
We may digest our complots in some form.
Exeunt.

Scene II. [London. Before Lord Hastings' house.]

Enter a *Messenger* to the door of *Hastings.*

Mess. My lord! my lord!
Hast. [*Within*] Who knocks?
Mess. One from the Lord Stanley.

Enter *Lord Hastings.*

Hast. What is't o'clock?
Mess. Upon the stroke of four. 5
Hast. Cannot my Lord Stanley sleep these tedious nights?
Mess. So it appears by that I have to say:
First, he commends him to your noble self.
Hast. What then? 10
Mess. Then certifies your lordship that this night
He dreamt the boar had rased off his helm:
Besides, he says there are two councils kept;
And that may be determined at the one
Which may make you and him to rue at the other. 15

26. **shallow:** trivial; slight; **instance:** proof; i.e., his fears are groundless.

Therefore he sends to know your lordship's pleasure,
If you will presently take horse with him
And with all speed post with him toward the North,
To shun the danger that his soul divines.
Hast. Go, fellow, go, return unto thy lord; 20
Bid him not fear the separated council.
His honor and myself are at the one,
And at the other is my good friend Catesby;
Where nothing can proceed that toucheth us
Whereof I shall not have intelligence. 25
Tell him his fears are shallow, without instance;
And for his dreams, I wonder he's so simple
To trust the mock'ry of unquiet slumbers.
To fly the boar before the boar pursues
Were to incense the boar to follow us, 30
And make pursuit where he did mean no chase.
Go, bid thy master rise and come to me,
And we will both together to the Tower,
Where he shall see the boar will use us kindly.
Mess. I'll go, my lord, and tell him what you say. 35
Exit.

Enter *Catesby.*

Cates. Many good morrows to my noble lord!
Hast. Good morrow, Catesby; you are early stirring.
What news, what news, in this our tott'ring state?
Cates. It is a reeling world indeed, my lord, 40
And I believe will never stand upright
Till Richard wear the garland of the realm.

46. **crown:** i.e., head.

50-2. **forward/ Upon his party:** in the vanguard of his supporters.

68. **send some packing:** dispatch some to their deaths.

72-4. **so 'twill do/ With some men else, that think themselves as safe/ As thou and I:** note the irony of Hastings' optimistic comments, which he little suspects hit close to his own fate.

Hast. How! wear the garland! Dost thou mean the crown?
Cates. Ay, my good lord. 45
Hast. I'll have this crown of mine cut from my shoulders
Before I'll see the crown so foul misplaced.
But canst thou guess that he doth aim at it?
Cates. Ay, on my life, and hopes to find you forward 50
Upon his party for the gain thereof;
And thereupon he sends you this good news,
That this same very day your enemies,
The kindred of the Queen, must die at Pomfret. 55
Hast. Indeed I am no mourner for that news,
Because they have been still my adversaries;
But that I'll give my voice on Richard's side
To bar my master's heirs in true descent,
God knows I will not do it, to the death! 60
Cates. God keep your lordship in that gracious mind!
Hast. But I shall laugh at this a twelvemonth hence,
That they which brought me in my master's hate, 65
I live to look upon their tragedy.
Well, Catesby, ere a fortnight make me older,
I'll send some packing that yet think not on't.
Cates. 'Tis a vile thing to die, my gracious lord,
When men are unprepared and look not for it. 70
Hast. O, monstrous, monstrous! and so falls it out
With Rivers, Vaughan, Grey; and so 'twill do
With some men else, that think themselves as safe

78. **account his head upon the Bridge:** plan on placing his head on London Bridge as that of an executed traitor.

85. **several:** separate.

96. **This sudden stab of rancor I misdoubt:** I am uneasy at the swiftness of this hostile act. Derby, no doubt, fears the fate of Rivers, Vaughan, and Grey should be a warning to all who may be in Richard's way.

99. **have with you:** let's go.

As thou and I, who, as thou knowst, are dear
To princely Richard and to Buckingham. 75
Cates. The princes both make high account of you—
[*Aside*] For they account his head upon the Bridge.
Hast. I know they do, and I have well deserved it.

Enter *Lord Stanley*, [*Earl of Derby*].

Come on, come on! Where is your boar-spear, man? 80
Fear you the boar, and go so unprovided?
Der. My lord, good morrow. Good morrow, Catesby.
You may jest on, but, by the Holy Rood,
I do not like these several councils, I. 85
Hast. My lord, I hold my life as dear as yours,
And never in my days, I do protest,
Was it so precious to me as 'tis now.
Think you, but that I know our state secure,
I would be so triumphant as I am? 90
Der. The lords at Pomfret, when they rode from London,
Were jocund and supposed their states were sure,
And they indeed had no cause to mistrust;
But yet you see how soon the day o'ercast. 95
This sudden stab of rancor I misdoubt:
Pray God, I say, I prove a needless coward!
What, shall we toward the Tower? The day is spent.
Hast. Come, come, have with you. Wot you what, my lord? 100
Today the lords you talked of are beheaded.

102-4. **They, for their truth, might better wear their heads/ Than some that have accused them wear their hats:** Rivers, Vaughan, and Grey better deserve to be alive than Richard and Buckingham deserve to have their places at the side of the Prince.

Ent. after l. 105. **Pursuivant:** a messenger of the state with the power to execute warrants.

116. **God hold it:** may God preserve your present state of fortune.

117. **Gramercy:** a corruption of the French *grand merci:* great thanks.

121. **Sir:** the clergy in general were honored with the title "Sir" on the basis that they should have taken their Bachelor of Arts degree at a university and thus earned the Latin title *dominus,* for which the English equivalent was "Sir."

122. **exercise:** sermon.

Der. They, for their truth, might better wear their heads
Than some that have accused them wear their hats.
But come, my lord, let's away. 105

Enter a *Pursuivant.*

Hast. Go on before. I'll talk with this good fellow.
Exeunt Lord Stanley, [Earl of Derby,] and Catesby.
How now, sirrah? How goes the world with thee?
Purs. The better that your lordship please to ask.
Hast. I tell thee, man, 'tis better with me now
Than when thou metst me last where now we meet. 110
Then was I going prisoner to the Tower
By the suggestion of the Queen's allies;
But now I tell thee—keep it to thyself—
This day those enemies are put to death,
And I in better state than e'er I was. 115
Purs. God hold it, to your honor's good content!
Hast. Gramercy, fellow. There, drink that for me.
Throws him his purse.
Purs. I thank your honor. *Exit Pursuivant.*

Enter a *Priest.*

Priest. Well met, my lord. I am glad to see your honor. 120
Hast. I thank thee, good Sir John, with all my heart.
I am in your debt for your last exercise;

123. **content:** gratify; reward.

128. **hath no shriving work in hand:** are not in need of final **shriving** (confession).

134. **stay:** stay for.

III. iii. Rivers, Vaughan, and Grey are led forth for execution. Rivers recalls Margaret of Anjou's curse on all those who had a part in her misfortunes and calls on God to see that Richard, Buckingham, and Hastings also feel its force.

Setting. **Pomfret Castle:** now known as Pontefract, a town in Yorkshire, containing the historic Norman castle where Richard II died. The castle was partially destroyed during the English Civil War.

Come the next Sabbath, and I will content you.

He whispers in his ear.

Priest. I'll wait upon your lordship.

Enter *Buckingham.*

Buck. What, talking with a priest, Lord Chamberlain? 125
Your friends at Pomfret, they do need the priest;
Your honor hath no shriving work in hand.

Hast. Good faith, and when I met this holy man,
The men you talk of came into my mind. 130
What, go you toward the Tower?

Buck. I do, my lord, but long I cannot stay there.
I shall return before your lordship thence.

Hast. Nay, like enough, for I stay dinner there.

Buck. [*Aside*] And supper too, although thou knowst it not.— 135
Come, will you go?

Hast. I'll wait upon your lordship.

Exeunt.

Scene III. [Pomfret Castle.]

Enter *Sir Richard Ratcliffe,* with *Halberds,* carrying the *Nobles,* [*Rivers, Grey,* and *Vaughan,*] to death at Pomfret.

Riv. Sir Richard Ratcliffe, let me tell thee this:
Today shalt thou behold a subject die
For truth, for duty, and for loyalty.

9. **The limit of your lives is out:** your allotted span of life is over.

12. **closure:** enclosure.

14. **for more slander to thy dismal seat:** as added shame to your ill-omened place. **Dismal** means literally "evil days," from the Latin *dies mali.*

27. **The hour of death is expiate:** that is, your last hour is come.

Sir Thomas Vaughan.
From a costume design by J. R. Planché (1829).

Grey. God bless the Prince from all the pack of you! 5
A knot you are of damned bloodsuckers.
Vaugh. You live that shall cry woe for this hereafter.
Rat. Dispatch! The limit of your lives is out.
Riv. O Pomfret, Pomfret! O thou bloody prison, 10
Fatal and ominous to noble peers!
Within the guilty closure of thy walls
Richard the Second here was hacked to death;
And, for more slander to thy dismal seat,
We give to thee our guiltless blood to drink. 15
Grey. Now Margaret's curse is fall'n upon our heads,
When she exclaimed on Hastings, you, and I,
For standing by when Richard stabbed her son.
Riv. Then cursed she Richard, then cursed she Buckingham, 20
Then cursed she Hastings. O, remember, God,
To hear her prayer for them, as now for us!
And for my sister and her princely sons,
Be satisfied, dear God, with our true blood, 25
Which, as thou knowst, unjustly must be spilt.
Rat. Make haste. The hour of death is expiate.
Riv. Come, Grey; come, Vaughan; let us here embrace.
Farewell, until we meet again in heaven. 30

Exeunt.

III. iv. Buckingham, Derby, Hastings, the Bishop of Ely, and several others hold a council meeting to make plans for Prince Edward's coronation. The confident Hastings announces that he can speak for the absent Richard, but at that moment the Duke himself enters. Hastings is confirmed in his optimism by Richard's gracious greeting, but is soon disillusioned when Richard accuses the Queen and Jane Shore of witchcraft and orders Hastings' execution as a traitor when he denies the possibility. Richard commands Ratcliffe to behead Hastings forthwith and allows him only a few moments for preparation.

5. **nomination:** naming of the day.
6. **happy:** favorable; opportune.

Scene IV. [London. The Tower.]

Enter *Buckingham,* [*Lord Stanley, Earl of*] *Derby,*
Hastings, Bishop of Ely, Norfolk, Ratcliffe, Lovel,
with others, at a table.

Hast. Now, noble peers, the cause why we are met
Is to determine of the coronation.
In God's name, speak. When is the royal day?
Buck. Is all things ready for the royal time?
Der. It is, and wants but nomination. 5
Ely. Tomorrow then I judge a happy day.
Buck. Who knows the Lord Protector's mind herein?
Who is most inward with the noble Duke?
Ely. Your Grace, we think, should soonest know his mind. 10
Buck. We know each other's faces; for our hearts,
He knows no more of mine than I of yours;
Or I of his, my lord, than you of mine.
Lord Hastings, you and he are near in love. 15
Hast. I thank his Grace, I know he loves me well;
But, for his purpose in the coronation,
I have not sounded him, nor he delivered
His gracious pleasure any way therein;
But you, my honorable lords, may name the time, 20
And in the Duke's behalf I'll give my voice,
Which, I presume, he'll take in gentle part.

23. **In happy time:** opportunely; see l. 6.
37. **Marry and will:** indeed I will.
42. **worshipfully:** dutifully.
43. **royalty:** sovereignty.
45-6. **triumph:** festive spectacle.

Enter [*Richard, Duke of*] *Gloucester.*

Ely. In happy time, here comes the Duke himself.
Rich. My noble lords and cousins all, good morrow.
I have been long a sleeper; but I trust 25
My absence doth neglect no great design
Which by my presence might have been concluded.
Buck. Had you not come upon your cue, my lord,
William Lord Hastings had pronounced your part—
I mean, your voice—for crowning of the King. 30
Rich. Than my Lord Hastings no man might be bolder.
His lordship knows me well, and loves me well.
My Lord of Ely, when I was last in Holborn
I saw good strawberries in your garden there. 35
I do beseech you send for some of them.
Ely. Marry and will, my lord, with all my heart.
Exit Bishop.
Rich. Cousin of Buckingham, a word with you.
[*Drawing him aside.*]
Catesby hath sounded Hastings in our business,
And finds the testy gentleman so hot 40
That he will lose his head ere give consent
His master's child, as worshipfully he terms it,
Shall lose the royalty of England's throne.
Buck. Withdraw yourself awhile. I'll go with you.
Exeunt [*Richard and Buckingham*].
Der. We have not yet set down this day of triumph: 45
Tomorrow, in my judgment, is too sudden;

49. **prolonged:** delayed.
54. **conceit:** idea; **likes:** pleases.
55. **When that:** when.

For I myself am not so well provided
As else I would be, were the day prolonged.

[Re-]enter the *Bishop of Ely.*

Ely. Where is my lord the Duke of Gloucester? 50
I have sent for these strawberries.
Hast. His Grace looks cheerfully and smooth this
morning;
There's some conceit or other likes him well
When that he bids good morrow with such spirit. 55
I think there's never a man in Christendom
Can lesser hide his love or hate than he,
For by his face straight shall you know his heart.
Der. What of his heart perceive you in his face
By any livelihood he showed today? 60
Hast. Marry, that with no man here he is offended;
For were he, he had shown it in his looks.

Enter *Richard* and *Buckingham.*

Rich. I pray you all, tell me what they deserve
That do conspire my death with devilish plots
Of damned witchcraft, and that have prevailed 65
Upon my body with their hellish charms.
Hast. The tender love I bear your Grace, my lord,
Makes me most forward in this princely presence
To doom the offenders, whosoe'er they be:
I say, my lord, they have deserved death. 70
Rich. Then be your eyes the witness of their evil.
Look how I am bewitched. Behold, mine arm

75. **Consorted:** associated.

79. **traitor:** historically, Richard executed Hastings for alleged complicity with the Queen and her relatives in a plot to abrogate Edward IV's will concerning the Protectorship.

85. **fond:** foolish.

88. **footcloth horse:** a horse with splendid trappings; **stumble:** an ill omen.

100. **shrift:** confession.

Is like a blasted sapling, withered up;
And this is Edward's wife, that monstrous witch,
Consorted with that harlot, strumpet Shore, 75
That by their witchcraft thus have marked me.

Hast. If they have done this deed, my noble lord—

Rich. If? Thou protector of this damned strumpet,
Talkst thou to me of ifs? Thou art a traitor.
Off with his head! Now, by Saint Paul I swear 80
I will not dine until I see the same.
Lovel and Ratcliffe, look that it be done:
The rest that love me, rise and follow me.

Exeunt. Manent Lovel and Ratcliffe, with the Lord Hastings.

Hast. Woe, woe for England, not a whit for me!
For I, too fond, might have prevented this. 85
Stanley did dream the boar did rase our helms;
But I did scorn it and disdain to fly.
Three times today my footcloth horse did stumble,
And started when he looked upon the Tower,
As loath to bear me to the slaughterhouse. 90
O, now I need the priest that spake to me!
I now repent I told the pursuivant,
As too triumphing, how mine enemies
Today at Pomfret bloodily were butchered,
And I myself secure in grace and favor. 95
O Margaret, Margaret, now thy heavy curse
Is lighted on poor Hastings' wretched head!

Rat. Come, come, dispatch! The Duke would be at dinner.
Make a short shrift; he longs to see your head. 100

Hast. O momentary grace of mortal men,

103. **in air of your good looks:** on the expectation of favor created by your kindly aspect.

107. **bootless:** profitless.

III. [v.] Richard and Buckingham report to the Mayor of London Hastings' execution because of a plot against their lives. When the Mayor leaves to tell the people about this deliverance from danger, Richard sends Buckingham after him to further their plans by hinting that Edward and his children were bastards. In the meantime, he intends to hide Clarence's children and give an order that no one is to see the princes in the Tower.

Ent. **rotten:** rusty; **ill-favored:** unsightly. This stage direction, which has Richard and Buckingham dress the part of men in fear of their lives, derives from Sir Thomas More's life of Richard III by way of Holinshed, where the description reads: ". . . at their coming, himselfe [Richard] with the duke of Buckingham stood harnessed in old ill faring briganders, such as no man should weene, that they would vouchsafe to haue put vpon their backs, except that some sudden necessitie had constreined them."

9. **Intending:** pretending.

11. **both are ready in their offices:** i.e., both **ghastly looks** and **enforced smiles** are ready for use.

Which we more hunt for than the grace of God!
Who builds his hope in air of your good looks
Lives like a drunken sailor on a mast,
Ready with every nod to tumble down 105
Into the fatal bowels of the deep.

Lov. Come, come, dispatch! 'Tis bootless to exclaim.

Hast. O bloody Richard! Miserable England!
I prophesy the fearfull'st time to thee 110
That ever wretched age hath looked upon.
Come, lead me to the block; bear him my head.
They smile at me who shortly shall be dead.

Exeunt.

[Scene V. London. The Tower walls.]

Enter *Richard,* [*Duke of Gloucester,*] and *Buckingham,* in rotten armor, marvelous ill-favored.

Rich. Come, cousin, canst thou quake, and change thy color,
Murder thy breath in middle of a word,
And then again begin, and stop again,
As if thou wert distraught and mad with terror? 5

Buck. Tut, I can counterfeit the deep tragedian,
Speak and look back, and pry on every side,
Tremble and start at wagging of a straw,
Intending deep suspicion: ghastly looks
Are at my service, like enforced smiles; 10
And both are ready in their offices,
At any time, to grace my stratagems.

27. **plainest harmless:** most plainly harmless.
29. **book:** diary.
32. **apparent open:** openly displayed.
33. **conversation:** amorous relationship.
34. **attainder of suspects:** attaint (stain) of suspicions.
35. **covert'st shelt'red:** most closely hidden.

But what, is Catesby gone?

Rich. He is; and see, he brings the Mayor along.

Enter the *Mayor* and *Catesby.*

Buck. Lord Mayor— 15

Rich. Look to the drawbridge there!

Buck. Hark! a drum.

Rich. Catesby, o'erlook the walls.

Buck. Lord Mayor, the reason we have sent—

Rich. Look back! defend thee! Here are enemies! 20

Buck. God and our innocency defend and guard us!

Enter *Lovel* and *Ratcliffe,* with *Hastings'* head.

Rich. Be patient, they are friends—Ratcliffe and Lovel.

Lov. Here is the head of that ignoble traitor,
The dangerous and unsuspected Hastings. 25

Rich. So dear I loved the man that I must weep:
I took him for the plainest harmless creature
That breathed upon the earth a Christian;
Made him my book, wherein my soul recorded
The history of all her secret thoughts. 30
So smooth he daubed his vice with show of virtue
That, his apparent open guilt omitted,
I mean, his conversation with Shore's wife,
He lived from all attainder of suspects.

Buck. Well, well, he was the covert'st shelt'red traitor 35

38. **almost:** even.

64. **Misconster us in him:** misconstrue our actions in thus dealing with him.

That ever lived.
Would you imagine, or almost believe,
Were't not that by great preservation
We live to tell it, that the subtle traitor 40
This day had plotted, in the council house,
To murder me and my good Lord of Gloucester?

May. Had he done so?

Rich. What? Think you we are Turks or infidels?
Or that we would, against the form of law, 45
Proceed thus rashly in the villain's death,
But that the extreme peril of the case,
The peace of England and our persons' safety,
Enforced us to this execution?

May. Now fair befall you! He deserved his death, 50
And your good Graces both have well proceeded
To warn false traitors from the like attempts.

Buck. I never looked for better at his hands
After he once fell in with Mistress Shore:
Yet had we not determined he should die 55
Until your lordship came to see his end,
Which now the loving haste of these our friends,
Something against our meanings, have prevented;
Because, my lord, I would have had you heard
The traitor speak, and timorously confess 60
The manner and the purpose of his treasons,
That you might well have signified the same
Unto the citizens, who haply may
Misconster us in him and wail his death.

May. But, my good lord, your Grace's words shall 65
serve,
As well as I had seen and heard him speak;

78. **hies him in all post:** hurries with all haste; see I. i. 158 and II. ii. 155.

79. **at your meet'st advantage:** at the most suitable opportunity.

80. **Infer:** allege; **the bastardy of Edward's children:** it was reported to Richard by the Bishop of Bath and Wells that Edward had engaged in a precontract with the Lady Eleanor Butler before his marriage to Elizabeth Woodville. Since such a precontract was as binding as marriage, it would have made his marriage to Elizabeth illegal and the children would have been illegitimate.

83. **the Crown:** a tavern owned by the citizen referred to.

85. **luxury:** lust.

88. **Even where:** wherever.

90. **for a need:** if necessary; if the rest is not sufficient to convince your hearers of my case.

91-2. **went with child/ Of that insatiate Edward:** i.e., when she bore Edward.

And do not doubt, right noble princes both,
But I'll acquaint our duteous citizens
With all your just proceedings in this case. 70

Rich. And to that end we wished your Lordship here,
T'avoid the censures of the carping world.

Buck. But since you come too late of our intent,
Yet witness what you hear we did intend: 75
And so, my good Lord Mayor, we bid farewell.

Exit Mayor.

Rich. Go after, after, cousin Buckingham.
The Mayor towards Guildhall hies him in all post:
There, at your meet'st advantage of the time,
Infer the bastardy of Edward's children. 80
Tell them how Edward put to death a citizen
Only for saying he would make his son
Heir to the Crown, meaning indeed his house,
Which by the sign thereof was termed so.
Moreover, urge his hateful luxury 85
And bestial appetite in change of lust,
Which stretched unto their servants, daughters, wives,
Even where his raging eye or savage heart,
Without control, lusted to make a prey.
Nay, for a need, thus far come near my person: 90
Tell them, when that my mother went with child
Of that insatiate Edward, noble York,
My princely father, then had wars in France,
And by true computation of the time
Found that the issue was not his begot; 95
Which well appeared in his lineaments,
Being nothing like the noble Duke my father.

101. **the golden fee:** that is, the crown.

103-4. **Baynard's Castle:** the London residence, on the Thames, of Richard's mother, the Duchess of York.

109-10. **Doctor Shaw . . . Friar Penker:** two popular preachers. Friar Ralph Shaw was actually the one who first spoke publicly of the alleged precontract.

113. **take some privy order:** make a secret arrangement.

III. [vi.] A scrivener contemplates the indictment of Lord Hastings, which is to be read in St. Paul's Cathedral to explain his execution. He thinks the charges against Hastings were obviously trumped up but that the temper of the time is such that no one will dare to say so.

---

3. **in a set hand fairly is engrossed:** is written clearly in a formal hand.

Yet touch this sparingly, as 'twere far off,
Because, my lord, you know my mother lives.
Buck. Doubt not, my lord, I'll play the orator 100
As if the golden fee for which I plead
Were for myself. And so, my lord, adieu.
Rich. If you thrive well, bring them to Baynard's Castle,
Where you shall find me well accompanied 105
With reverend fathers and well-learned bishops.
Buck. I go; and towards three or four o'clock
Look for the news that the Guildhall affords.
Exit Buckingham.
Rich. Go, Lovel, with all speed to Doctor Shaw—
[*To Catesby*] Go thou to Friar Penker.—Bid them both 110
Meet me within this hour at Baynard's Castle.
Exeunt [*Lovel, Catesby, and Ratcliffe*].
Now will I go to take some privy order
To draw the brats of Clarence out of sight,
And to give order that no manner person 115
Have any time recourse unto the princes.
Exit.

[Scene VI. London. A street.]

Enter a *Scrivener* with a paper in his hand.

Scriv. Here is the indictment of the good Lord Hastings,
Which in a set hand fairly is engrossed

5. **sequel:** sequence of events.

8. **precedent:** draft of the indictment.

10. **Untainted:** unattainted; uncharged with treason.

11. **the while:** this present time; **gross:** stupid.

12. **palpable device:** obvious contrivance.

15. **seen in thought:** i.e., only in thought; observed but not mentioned.

III. [vii.] Buckingham reports to Richard the success of the suggestion that Edward and his children are illegitimate and that Richard is the only rightful heir to the throne. Though no great enthusiasm was provoked by these disclosures, the Mayor has come to ask Richard to consent to reign. Buckingham and Richard arrange a show of piety and reluctance to assume this responsibility, but Richard at length condescends to yield to the Mayor's pleas. It is decided that he will be crowned the next day.

6. **Lady Lucy:** Elizabeth Lucy, an old mistress of Edward IV before his marriage. The precontract, however, if it existed at all, was not with her. See note at III. [v.] 80.

7. **his contract by deputy in France:** i.e., with the Lady Bona of Savoy, sister-in-law of Louis IX. The Earl of Warwick had negotiated with the French King for this alliance, but Edward in the meantime was coming to an agreement with Elizabeth Woodville.

That it may be today read o'er in Paul's.
And mark how well the sequel hangs together: 5
Eleven hours I have spent to write it over,
For yesternight by Catesby was it sent me;
The precedent was full as long a-doing;
And yet within these five hours Hastings lived,
Untainted, unexamined, free, at liberty. 10
Here's a good world the while! Who is so gross
That cannot see this palpable device?
Yet who so bold but says he sees it not?
Bad is the world, and all will come to nought
When such ill dealing must be seen in thought. 15
Exit.

[Scene VII. London. Baynard's Castle.]

Enter *Richard*, [*Duke of Gloucester*,] and *Buckingham* at several doors.

Rich. How now, how now, what say the citizens?
Buck. Now, by the holy Mother of our Lord,
The citizens are mum, say not a word.
Rich. Touched you the bastardy of Edward's children? 5
Buck. I did, with his contract with Lady Lucy
And his contract by deputy in France;
The unsatiate greediness of his desire
And his enforcement of the city wives;
His tyranny for trifles; his own bastardy, 10
As being got, your father then in France,

12. **resemblance:** that is, semblance; appearance.

13. **infer your lineaments:** point out your features.

14. **right idea:** true image.

31. **the Recorder:** originally a man of some legal knowledge appointed by the Mayor or Aldermen to record facts and recite them orally when necessary as evidence of the truth.

34. **nothing spake in warrant from himself:** added nothing in support of the facts alleged.

And his resemblance, being not like the Duke.
Withal I did infer your lineaments,
Being the right idea of your father
Both in your form and nobleness of mind; 15
Laid open all your victories in Scotland,
Your discipline in war, wisdom in peace,
Your bounty, virtue, fair humility;
Indeed, left nothing fitting for your purpose
Untouched or slightly handled in discourse; 20
And when my oratory drew toward end,
I bid them that did love their country's good
Cry, "God save Richard, England's royal King!"
Rich. And did they so?
Buck. No, so God help me, they spake not a word, 25
But, like dumb statuës or breathing stones,
Stared each on other, and looked deadly pale.
Which when I saw, I reprehended them
And asked the Mayor what meant this willful silence.
His answer was, the people were not used 30
To be spoke to but by the Recorder.
Then he was urged to tell my tale again:
"Thus saith the Duke, thus hath the Duke inferred,"—
But nothing spake in warrant from himself.
When he had done, some followers of mine own, 35
At lower end of the hall, hurled up their caps,
And some ten voices cried, "God save King Richard!"
And thus I took the vantage of those few:
"Thanks, gentle citizens and friends," quoth I.
"This general applause and cheerful shout 40
Argues your wisdoms and your love to Richard."—
And even here brake off and came away.

48. **Intend:** pretend; see III. [v.] 9.

50. **by mighty suit:** after much pleading.

53. **For on that ground I'll make a holy descant:** that is, on the basis of Richard's companionship of clergymen he will **descant** on Richard's piety. See **descant,** I. i. 27.

59. **leads:** i.e., the roof, which was covered with lead sheets.

61. **dance attendance:** i.e., kick my heels. Buckingham wants to give the impression that he has been waiting a long time without gaining admission to Richard.

Rich. What tongueless blocks were they! Would they not speak?
Buck. No, by my troth, my lord. 45
Rich. Will not the Mayor then and his brethren come?
Buck. The Mayor is here at hand. Intend some fear;
Be not you spoke with but by mighty suit; 50
And look you get a prayer book in your hand
And stand between two churchmen, good my lord,
For on that ground I'll make a holy descant.
And be not easily won to our requests;
Play the maid's part: still answer nay, and take it. 55
Rich. I go; and if you plead as well for them
As I can say nay to thee for myself,
No doubt we bring it to a happy issue.
Buck. Go, go, up to the leads! The Lord Mayor knocks. 60
[*Exit Richard.*]

Enter the *Mayor*, [*Aldermen,*] and *Citizens.*

Welcome, my lord. I dance attendance here;
I think the Duke will not be spoke withal.

Enter *Catesby.*

Now, Catesby, what says your lord to my request?
Cates. He doth entreat your Grace, my noble lord,
To visit him tomorrow or next day: 65
He is within, with two right reverend fathers,
Divinely bent to meditation,

77. **lulling:** lolling.
81. **engross:** fatten.
86. **defend:** forbid.

And in no worldly suits would he be moved
To draw him from his holy exercise.
Buck. Return, good Catesby, to the gracious Duke: 70
Tell him, myself, the Mayor and Aldermen,
In deep designs, in matter of great moment,
No less importing than our general good,
Are come to have some conference with his Grace.
Cates. I'll signify so much unto him straight. *Exit.* 75
Buck. Ah ha, my lord, this prince is not an Edward!
He is not lulling on a lewd love-bed,
But on his knees at meditation;
Not dallying with a brace of courtesans,
But meditating with two deep divines; 80
Not sleeping, to engross his idle body,
But praying, to enrich his watchful soul.
Happy were England, would this virtuous prince
Take on his Grace the sovereignty thereof;
But sure I fear we shall not win him to it. 85
May. Marry, God defend his Grace should say us nay!
Buck. I fear he will. Here Catesby comes again.

[Re-]enter *Catesby.*

Now, Catesby, what says his Grace?
Cates. He wonders to what end you have assembled 90
Such troops of citizens to come to him,
His Grace not being warned thereof before:
He fears, my lord, you mean no good to him.
Buck. Sorry I am my noble cousin should
Suspect me that I mean no good to him: 95

104. **fall of vanity:** falling into worldly frivolity.
120. **disgracious:** ungracious; displeasing.

By heaven, we come to him in perfect love;
And so once more return and tell his Grace.
Exit [Catesby].
When holy and devout religious men
Are at their beads, 'tis much to draw them thence,
So sweet is zealous contemplation. 100

Enter *Richard* aloft, between two *Bishops*.
[*Catesby returns.*]

May. See where his Grace stands, 'tween two clergymen.
Buck. Two props of virtue for a Christian prince,
To stay him from the fall of vanity;
And see, a book of prayer in his hand— 105
True ornaments to know a holy man.
Famous Plantagenet, most gracious prince,
Lend favorable ear to our requests,
And pardon us the interruption
Of thy devotion and right Christian zeal. 110
Rich. My lord, there needs no such apology:
I do beseech your Grace to pardon me,
Who, earnest in the service of my God,
Deferred the visitation of my friends.
But, leaving this, what is your Grace's pleasure? 115
Buck. Even that, I hope, which pleaseth God above,
And all good men of this ungoverned isle.
Rich. I do suspect I have done some offense
That seems disgracious in the city's eye, 120
And that you come to reprehend my ignorance.

134. **proper:** own.

136. **graft:** grafted. The form **graft** is the early form of the word, the participle of the verb "to graff."

137. **in:** into.

139. **recure:** heal again.

143. **factor:** agent.

144. **successively:** by right of succession.

145. **empery:** empire.

147. **worshipful:** respectful.

Buck. You have, my lord. Would it might please your Grace,
On our entreaties, to amend your fault!
Rich. Else wherefore breathe I in a Christian land? 125
Buck. Know then, it is your fault that you resign
The supreme seat, the throne majestical,
The scept'red office of your ancestors,
Your state of fortune and your due of birth,
The lineal glory of your royal house, 130
To the corruption of a blemished stock;
Whiles, in the mildness of your sleepy thoughts,
Which here we waken to our country's good,
The noble isle doth want her proper limbs;
Her face defaced with scars of infamy, 135
Her royal stock graft with ignoble plants,
And almost should'red in the swallowing gulf
Of dark forgetfulness and deep oblivion.
Which to recure, we heartily solicit
Your gracious self to take on you the charge 140
And kingly government of this your land;
Not as Protector, steward, substitute,
Or lowly factor for another's gain;
But as successively, from blood to blood,
Your right of birth, your empery, your own. 145
For this, consorted with the citizens,
Your very worshipful and loving friends,
And by their vehement instigation,
In this just cause come I to move your Grace.
Rich. I cannot tell if to depart in silence, 150
Or bitterly to speak in your reproof,
Best fitteth my degree or your condition.

156. **fondly:** foolishly.

159. **checked:** rebuked.

162. **Definitively:** finally.

166. **even:** regular; free of obstacles.

167. **As the ripe revenue and due of birth:** i.e., the inheritance that should now come to me by right of birth.

168. **poverty of spirit:** humility; probably Richard means to claim for himself membership among the "poor in spirit" blessed in the Bible.

171. **brook:** endure; see I. i. 136 and I. iii. 4.

177. **stealing:** i.e., overtaking imperceptibly. In short, Richard implies that the Prince of Wales will be old enough to rule before they know it.

If not to answer, you might haply think
Tongue-tied ambition, not replying, yielded
To bear the golden yoke of sovereignty 155
Which fondly you would here impose on me.
If to reprove you for this suit of yours,
So seasoned with your faithful love to me,
Then, on the other side, I checked my friends.
Therefore, to speak, and to avoid the first, 160
And then, in speaking, not to incur the last,
Definitively thus I answer you.
Your love deserves my thanks, but my desert
Unmeritable shuns your high request.
First, if all obstacles were cut away, 165
And that my path were even to the crown
As the ripe revenue and due of birth,
Yet so much is my poverty of spirit,
So mighty and so many my defects,
That I would rather hide me from my greatness, 170
Being a bark to brook no mighty sea,
Than in my greatness covet to be hid
And in the vapor of my glory smothered.
But, God be thanked, there is no need of me,
And much I need to help you, were there need: 175
The royal tree hath left us royal fruit,
Which, mellowed by the stealing hours of time,
Will well become the seat of majesty,
And make, no doubt, us happy by his reign.
On him I lay that you would lay on me, 180
The right and fortune of his happy stars,
Which God defend that I should wring from him!

185. **respects:** considerations; **nice:** almost synonymous with **trivial:** magnified by being examined too minutely.

191. **substitute:** proxy.

193. **petitioner:** Shakespeare portrays Elizabeth's appeal to Edward IV for the restoration of her dead husband's lands in III. ii. of *Henry VI, Part III.*

197. **Made prize and purchase of:** seized upon as a prize.

198. **the pitch and height of his degree: pitch** is a term from hawking meaning the highest point of the hawk's flight before stooping to his prey, and therefore it accentuates the word **height.**

199. **base declension:** a decline into a lower condition.

202. **expostulate:** relate in detail.

Edward IV and Prince Edward.
From a costume design by J. R. Planché (1829).

Buck. My lord, this argues conscience in your Grace.
But the respects thereof are nice and trivial, 185
All circumstances well considered.
You say that Edward is your brother's son:
So say we too, but not by Edward's wife;
For first was he contract to Lady Lucy—
Your mother lives a witness to his vow— 190
And afterward by substitute betrothed
To Bona, sister to the King of France.
These both put off, a poor petitioner,
A care-crazed mother to a many sons,
A beauty-waning and distressed widow, 195
Even in the afternoon of her best days,
Made prize and purchase of his wanton eye,
Seduced the pitch and height of his degree
To base declension and loathed bigamy.
By her, in his unlawful bed, he got 200
This Edward, whom our manners call the Prince.
More bitterly could I expostulate,
Save that, for reverence to some alive,
I give a sparing limit to my tongue.
Then, good my lord, take to your royal self 205
This proffered benefit of dignity;
If not to bless us and the land withal,
Yet to draw forth your noble ancestry
From the corruption of abusing times
Unto a lineal true-derived course. 210

May. Do, good my lord; your citizens entreat you.
Buck. Refuse not, mighty lord, this proffered love.
Cates. O make them joyful, grant their lawful suit!

221. **kind:** natural; **effeminate remorse:** compassionate pity.

223. **egally:** equally.

224. **whe'er:** whether.

Rich. Alas, why would you heap this care on me?
I am unfit for state and majesty: 215
I do beseech you, take it not amiss,
I cannot nor I will not yield to you.
Buck. If you refuse it—as, in love and zeal,
Loath to depose the child, your brother's son;
As well we know your tenderness of heart 220
And gentle, kind, effeminate remorse,
Which we have noted in you to your kindred
And egally indeed to all estates—
Yet know, whe'er you accept our suit or no,
Your brother's son shall never reign our king, 225
But we will plant some other in the throne,
To the disgrace and downfall of your house;
And in this resolution here we leave you.
Come, citizens. Zounds, I'll entreat no more!
Rich. O do not swear, my lord of Buckingham. 230
Exeunt [*all but Richard and Catesby*].
Cates. Call him again, sweet prince, accept their suit:
If you deny them, all the land will rue it.
Rich. Will you enforce me to a world of cares?
Call them again. I am not made of stones, 235
But penetrable to your kind entreaties,
Albeit against my conscience and my soul.

[Re-]enter *Buckingham* and the rest.

Cousin of Buckingham, and sage, grave men,
Since you will buckle fortune on my back,
To bear her burden, whe'er I will or no, 240

243. **imposition:** i.e., the burden they force him to assume.

244. **mere:** sheer, downright; that is, the fact that they absolutely forced him; **acquittance:** acquit.

I must have patience to endure the load;
But if black scandal or foul-faced reproach
Attend the sequel of your imposition,
Your mere enforcement shall acquittance me
From all the impure blots and stains thereof; 245
For God doth know, and you may partly see,
How far I am from the desire of this.
May. God bless your Grace! We see it and will say it.
Rich. In saying so you shall but say the truth. 250
Buck. Then I salute you with this royal title—
Long live King Richard, England's worthy King!
All. Amen.
Buck. Tomorrow may it please you to be crowned?
Rich. Even when you please, for you will have it so. 255
Buck. Tomorrow then we will attend your Grace,
And so most joyfully we take our leave.
Rich. [*To the Bishops*] Come, let us to our holy work again.— 260
Farewell, my cousin; farewell, gentle friends.

Exeunt.

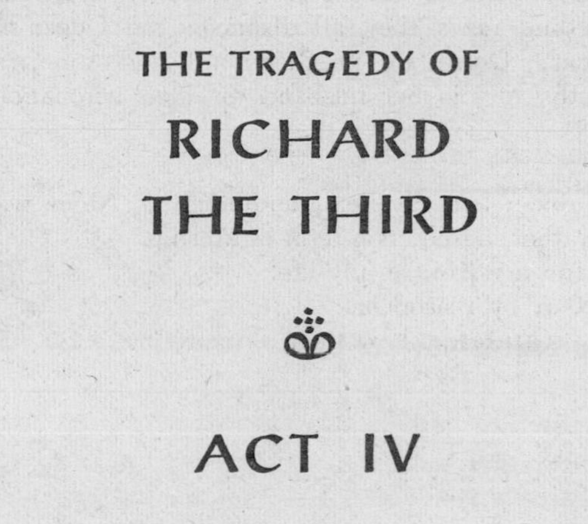

THE TRAGEDY OF RICHARD THE THIRD

ACT IV

IV. i. Queen Elizabeth, with the Duchess of York and the Marquess of Dorset, meets Richard's wife, Anne, escorting Clarence's daughter Margaret, at the Tower of London, where they have all come to visit the princes. They soon learn that Richard, styled the King by the Lieutenant of the Tower, has forbidden anyone to have access to the boys. At this foreboding news they all disperse: the Queen to sanctuary; Dorset to join Richmond; and Anne, reluctantly, to join her husband for their coronation.

1. **niece:** actually her granddaughter. **Niece** was used rather loosely as a term of kinship.

3. **for my life:** on my life.

4. **On:** by reason of.

12. **gratulate:** show their pleasure in.

ACT IV

Scene I. [London. Outside the Tower.]

Enter the *Queen* [*Elizabeth*], the *Duchess of York,* and *Marquess* [*of*] *Dorset* [at one door]; *Anne, Duchess of Gloucester,* [*Lady Margaret Plantagenet, Clarence's* daughter, at another door].

Duch. Who meets us here? My niece Plantagenet,
Led in the hand of her kind aunt of Gloucester?
Now, for my life, she's wand'ring to the Tower
On pure heart's love, to greet the tender Prince.
Daughter, well met. 5

Anne. God give your Graces both
A happy and a joyful time of day!

Queen. As much to you, good sister. Whither away?

Anne. No farther than the Tower, and, as I guess, 10
Upon the like devotion as yourselves,
To gratulate the gentle princes there.

Queen. Kind sister, thanks. We'll enter all together.

Enter the *Lieutenant* [*Brakenbury*].

And in good time, here the Lieutenant comes.
Master Lieutenant, pray you, by your leave, 15
How doth the Prince, and my young son of York?

18. **suffer:** allow.

29. **take thy office from thee:** assume your function as their guardian.

30. **it:** i.e., his office.

38. **lace:** i.e., the tight lacing of her bodice. The fashion of Shakespeare's time decreed an artificially constricted waistline for both men and women.

Anne, Queen of Richard III.
From a costume design by J. R. Planché (1829).

Lieut. Right well, dear madam. By your patience,
I may not suffer you to visit them;
The King hath strictly charged the contrary.
Queen. The King? Who's that? 20
Lieut. I mean the Lord Protector.
Queen. The Lord protect him from that kingly title!
Hath he set bounds between their love and me?
I am their mother; who shall bar me from them? 25
Duch. I am their father's mother; I will see them.
Anne. Their aunt I am in law, in love their mother;
Then bring me to their sights. I'll bear thy blame
And take thy office from thee on my peril.
Lieut. No, madam, no! I may not leave it so: 30
I am bound by oath, and therefore pardon me.
Exit Lieutenant.

Enter *Stanley,* [*Earl of Derby*].

Der. Let me but meet you, ladies, one hour hence,
And I'll salute your Grace of York as mother
And reverend looker-on of two fair queens.
[*To Anne*] Come, madam, you must straight to Westminster, 35
There to be crowned Richard's royal queen.
Queen. Ah, cut my lace asunder,
That my pent heart may have some scope to beat,
Or else I swoon with this dead-killing news! 40
Anne. Despiteful tidings! O unpleasing news!
Dor. Be of good cheer. Mother, how fares your Grace?

47-8. **go cross the seas,/ And live with Richmond:** Richmond (Henry Tudor) had taken refuge in France after the Battle of Tewkesbury.

52. **counted:** accounted; i.e., acknowledged.

60. **cockatrice:** another legendary creature often confused with the **basilisk;** see I. ii. 174.

64-5. **inclusive verge/ Of golden metal:** encircling royal crown of gold.

67. **deadly venom:** i.e., instead of the holy oil normally used in coronation ceremonies.

Queen. O Dorset, speak not to me, get thee gone!
Death and destruction dogs thee at thy heels; 45
Thy mother's name is ominous to children.
If thou wilt outstrip death, go cross the seas,
And live with Richmond, from the reach of hell.
Go hie thee, hie thee from this slaughterhouse,
Lest thou increase the number of the dead 50
And make me die the thrall of Margaret's curse,
Nor mother, wife, nor England's counted Queen.
Der. Full of wise care is this your counsel, madam:
Take all the swift advantage of the hours.
You shall have letters from me to my son 55
In your behalf, to meet you on the way:
Be not ta'en tardy by unwise delay.
Duch. O ill-dispersing wind of misery!
O my accursed womb, the bed of death!
A cockatrice hast thou hatched to the world, 60
Whose unavoided eye is murderous.
Der. Come, madam, come! I in all haste was sent.
Anne. And I with all unwillingness will go.
O would to God that the inclusive verge
Of golden metal that must round my brow 65
Were red-hot steel, to sear me to the brains!
Anointed let me be with deadly venom
And die, ere men can say, "God save the Queen!"
Queen. Go, go, poor soul! I envy not thy glory.
To feed my humor wish thyself no harm. 70
Anne. No? Why! when he that is my husband now
Came to me as I followed Henry's corse,
When scarce the blood was well washed from his
hands

79. **so old a widow:** a widow for so long a period, since she was so young when her husband died.

86. **Grossly:** stupidly; see III. [vi.] 11.

88. **hitherto:** ever since.

Which issued from my other angel husband 75
And that dear saint which then I weeping followed—
O, when, I say, I looked on Richard's face,
This was my wish: "Be thou," quoth I, "accursed
For making me, so young, so old a widow!
And when thou wedst, let sorrow haunt thy bed; 80
And be thy wife, if any be so mad,
More miserable by the death of thee
Than thou hast made me by my dear lord's death!"
Lo, ere I can repeat this curse again,
Within so small a time, my woman's heart 85
Grossly grew captive to his honey words
And proved the subject of mine own soul's curse,
Which hitherto hath held mine eyes from rest;
For never yet one hour in his bed
Did I enjoy the golden dew of sleep, 90
But with his timorous dreams was still awaked.
Besides, he hates me for my father Warwick,
And will, no doubt, shortly be rid of me.

Queen. Poor heart, adieu! I pity thy complaining.

Anne. No more than with my soul I mourn for yours. 95

Dor. Farewell, thou woeful welcomer of glory.

Anne. Adieu, poor soul, that takest thy leave of it.

Duch. [*To Dorset*] Go thou to Richmond, and good fortune guide thee!
[*To Anne*] Go thou to Richard, and good angels tend thee! 100
[*To Queen*] Go thou to sanctuary, and good thoughts possess thee!
I to my grave, where peace and rest lie with me!

106. **wracked:** wrecked; **teen:** misery.
110. **envy:** malice; **immured:** shut up.

IV. ii. Richard, now King, suggests to Buckingham the desirability of disposing of his nephews in the Tower. Buckingham asks time to think it over and Richard begins to fear that he can no longer rely on Buckingham's wholehearted support. He hires James Tyrrel to kill the boys and lays the groundwork to dispose of his wife so that he can marry Edward's daughter as double insurance for his hold on the throne.

When Buckingham returns, he asks for the fulfillment of Richard's promise concerning the earldom of Hereford and the movable possessions of Edward IV, but Richard replies that he is not in a giving vein and his manner is such that Buckingham decides to flee before he meets Hastings' fate.

Ent. **sennet:** a series of trumpet notes announcing the arrival of royalty or nobility.

9. **touch:** touchstone, to test the genuineness of gold.

Eighty odd years of sorrow have I seen, 105
And each hour's joy wracked with a week of teen.

Queen. Stay, yet look back with me unto the Tower.
Pity, you ancient stones, those tender babes
Whom envy hath immured within your walls, 110
Rough cradle for such little pretty ones!
Rude ragged nurse, old sullen playfellow
For tender princes, use my babies well!
So foolish sorrow bids your stones farewell.

Exeunt.

Scene II. [London. The Palace.]

Sound a sennet. Enter *Richard,* in pomp, *Buckingham, Catesby, Ratcliffe, Lovel,* [a *Page,* and others].

Rich. Stand all apart. Cousin of Buckingham—

Buck. My gracious sovereign?

Rich. Give me thy hand.

Sound. Here he ascendeth the throne.

Thus high, by thy advice
And thy assistance, is King Richard seated: 5
But shall we wear these glories for a day?
Or shall they last, and we rejoice in them?

Buck. Still live they, and for ever let them last!

Rich. Ah, Buckingham, now do I play the touch,
To try if thou be current gold indeed: 10
Young Edward lives. Think now what I would speak.

Buck. Say on, my loving lord.

18. **live true noble Prince:** i.e., remain the legitimate heir to the throne.

26. **breath:** breathing time.

29. **resolve you herein presently:** satisfy you in the matter at once.

32. **iron-witted:** insensitive.

33. **unrespective:** heedless; not given to thoughtful consideration.

34. **considerate:** thoughtful.

39. **close:** secret.

A king in pomp.
From an 1883 reprint of *Caxton's Game and Playe of the Chesse* (1474).

Rich. Why, Buckingham, I say I would be King.
Buck. Why, so you are, my thrice-renowned liege.
Rich. Ha! Am I King? 'Tis so. But Edward lives. 15
Buck. True, noble prince.
Rich. O bitter consequence,
That Edward still should live true noble Prince!
Cousin, thou wast not wont to be so dull.
Shall I be plain? I wish the bastards dead, 20
And I would have it suddenly performed.
What sayst thou now? Speak suddenly, be brief.
Buck. Your Grace may do your pleasure.
Rich. Tut, tut, thou art all ice; thy kindness freezes.
Say, have I thy consent that they shall die? 25
Buck. Give me some little breath, some pause, dear lord,
Before I positively speak in this:
I will resolve you herein presently.
Exit Buck[*ingham*].
Cates. [*Aside to a bystander*] The King is angry. 30
See, he gnaws his lip.
Rich. I will converse with iron-witted fools
And unrespective boys. None are for me
That look into me with considerate eyes.
High reaching Buckingham grows circumspect. 35
Boy!
Page. My lord?
Rich. Knowst thou not any whom corrupting gold
Will tempt unto a close exploit of death?
Page. I know a discontented gentleman 40
Whose humble means match not his haughty spirit:

47. **deep-revolving:** i.e., prone to turning over in his mind every possible aspect of a situation; **witty:** cunning.

56. **grievous:** severely; distressingly.

57. **for her keeping close:** that is, that she be kept close (imprisoned).

60. **foolish:** dim-witted.

63. **stands me much upon:** is extremely important for me.

65. **my brother's daughter:** Edward IV's daughter Elizabeth, who later married Henry Tudor.

Gold were as good as twenty orators,
And will, no doubt, tempt him to anything.
Rich. What is his name?
Page. His name, my lord, is Tyrrel. 45
Rich. I partly know the man. Go call him hither.
Exit [*Page*].
The deep-revolving witty Buckingham
No more shall be the neighbor to my counsels.
Hath he so long held out with me untired,
And stops he now for breath? Well, be it so. 50

Enter *Stanley,* [*Earl of Derby*].

How now, Lord Stanley? What's the news?
Der. Know, my loving lord,
The Marquess Dorset, as I hear, is fled
To Richmond in the parts where he abides.
[*Stands apart.*]
Rich. Come hither, Catesby. Rumor it abroad 55
That Anne my wife is very grievous sick:
I will take order for her keeping close.
Inquire me out some mean poor gentleman,
Whom I will marry straight to Clarence' daughter.
The boy is foolish, and I fear not him. 60
Look how thou dreamst! I say again, give out
That Anne my queen is sick and like to die.
About it! for it stands me much upon
To stop all hopes whose growth may damage me.
[*Exit Catesby.*]
I must be married to my brother's daughter, 65
Or else my kingdom stands on brittle glass:

69. **pluck on:** incite.
74. **Prove:** test.
76. **Please you:** as you please.
87. **There is no more but so:** that's all there is to it.
88. **prefer:** promote.

Murder her brothers, and then marry her—
Uncertain way of gain! But I am in
So far in blood that sin will pluck on sin.
Tear-falling pity dwells not in this eye. 70

Enter [*Page,* with] *Tyrrel.*

Is thy name Tyrrel?
Tyr. James Tyrrel, and your most obedient subject.
Rich. Art thou indeed?
Tyr. Prove me, my gracious lord.
Rich. Darest thou resolve to kill a friend of mine? 75
Tyr. Please you;
But I had rather kill two enemies.
Rich. Why then thou hast it! Two deep enemies,
Foes to my rest and my sweet sleep's disturbers,
Are they that I would have thee deal upon: 80
Tyrrel, I mean those bastards in the Tower.
Tyr. Let me have open means to come to them,
And soon I'll rid you from the fear of them.
Rich. Thou singst sweet music. Hark, come hither,
Tyrrel. 85
Go, by this token. Rise, and lend thine ear. (*Whispers.*)
There is no more but so: say it is done,
And I will love thee and prefer thee for it.
Tyr. I will dispatch it straight. *Exit.*

[Re-]enter *Buckingham.*

Buck. My lord, I have considered in my mind 90
The late request that you did sound me in.

95. **he:** i.e., Richmond. His mother, Margaret Beaufort, was now married to Thomas, Lord Stanley; see I. iii. 25.

Rich. Well, let that rest. Dorset is fled to Richmond.

Buck. I hear the news, my lord.

Rich. Stanley, he is your wife's son. Well, look unto it. 95

Buck. My lord, I claim the gift, my due by promise,
For which your honor and your faith is pawned:
The earldom of Hereford and the movables
Which you have promised I shall possess. 100

Rich. Stanley, look to your wife: if she convey
Letters to Richmond, you shall answer it.

Buck. What says your Highness to my just request?

Rich. I do remember me Henry the Sixth
Did prophesy that Richmond should be King 105
When Richmond was a little peevish boy.
A king!—perhaps—perhaps—

Buck. My lord—

Rich. How chance the prophet could not at that time 110
Have told me, I being by, that I should kill him?

Buck. My lord, your promise for the earldom!

Rich. Richmond! When last I was at Exeter,
The Mayor in courtesy showed me the castle,
And called it Rouge-mount; at which name I started, 115
Because a bard of Ireland told me once
I should not live long after I saw Richmond.

Buck. My lord—

Rich. Ay, what's o'clock?

Buck. I am thus bold to put your Grace in mind 120
Of what you promised me.

Rich. Well, but what's o'clock?

126-27. **Jack:** mechanical figure in the shape of a man that pantomimed the action of striking in time to the actual striking of the clock. There is also an insulting play on **Jack** meaning an ill-bred knave; see I. iii. 63, 83; **keepst the stroke:** i.e., sound the same note with mechanical regularity.

129. **the giving vein:** the mood for giving.

135. **Brecknock:** Brecon, in South Wales, where Buckingham had a residence.

IV. [iii.] Richard receives word that the murder of the princes has been carried out. With Clarence's son imprisoned, his daughter married to an obscure and powerless man, Edward's sons dead, and Richard's wife, Anne, also out of the way, the next step is to seek the hand of his niece Elizabeth, whom Richmond also hopes to marry. But Richard's complacent reflections are shortly interrupted by Ratcliffe, who reports that the Bishop of Ely has escaped and fled to join Richmond, and that Buckingham has a large army in the field in revolt against Richard.

---

1. **tyrannous:** violent.

2. **most arch:** greatest.

4. **suborn:** bribe.

6. **fleshed:** hardened. Dogs and hawks were trained to hunt by being **fleshed** (given a taste of the flesh of the game hunted).

8. **in their deaths' sad story:** i.e., in telling the sad story of their deaths.

Buck. Upon the stroke of ten.
Rich. Well, let it strike.
Buck. Why let it strike? 125
Rich. Because that, like a Jack, thou keepst the stroke
Betwixt thy begging and my meditation.
I am not in the giving vein today.
Buck. May it please you to resolve me in my suit. 130
Rich. Thou troublest me; I am not in the vein.
Exeunt [*all but Buckingham*].
Buck. And is it thus? Repays he my deep service
With such contempt? Made I him King for this?
O let me think on Hastings, and be gone
To Brecknock while my fearful head is on! 135
Exit.

Scene [III. London. The Palace.]

Enter *Tyrrel.*

Tyr. The tyrannous and bloody act is done,
The most arch deed of piteous massacre
That ever yet this land was guilty of.
Dighton and Forrest, who I did suborn
To do this piece of ruthless butchery, 5
Albeit they were fleshed villains, bloody dogs,
Melted with tenderness and mild compassion,
Wept like to children in their deaths' sad story.
"O, thus," quoth Dighton, "lay the gentle babes."

11. **alablaster:** alabaster (white).

19. **replenished:** plentifully supplied with virtues.

20. **prime:** first.

34. **after-supper:** reresupper, a light meal set out when the main supper was over.

35. **process:** story.

Richard III.
From an 1811 reprint of John Rastell, *The Pastime of People* (1529).

"Thus, thus," quoth Forrest, "girdling one another 10
Within their alablaster innocent arms.
Their lips were four red roses on a stalk,
And in their summer beauty kissed each other.
A book of prayers on their pillow lay,
Which once," quoth Forrest, "almost changed my 15
mind;
But O! the Devil"—there the villain stopped;
When Dighton thus told on—"We smothered
The most replenished sweet work of nature
That from the prime creation e'er she framed." 20
Hence both are gone with conscience and remorse:
They could not speak; and so I left them both,
To bear this tidings to the bloody King.

Enter [*King*] *Richard.*

And here he comes. All health, my sovereign lord!
Rich. Kind Tyrrel, am I happy in thy news? 25
Tyr. If to have done the thing you gave in charge
Beget your happiness, be happy then,
For it is done.
Rich. But didst thou see them dead?
Tyr. I did, my lord. 30
Rich. And buried, gentle Tyrrel?
Tyr. The chaplain of the Tower hath buried them;
But where, to say the truth, I do not know.
Rich. Come to me, Tyrrel, soon at after-supper,
When thou shalt tell the process of their death. 35
Meantime, but think how I may do thee good,

44. **for:** because; **Britain:** i.e., Breton. Richmond was living in Brittany.

46. **by that knot looks proudly on the crown:** by means of that alliance hopes to account the crown his own.

51. **Morton:** the Bishop of Ely, who had been in Buckingham's custody since his conspiracy with Hastings became known.

57-8. **fearful commenting/ Is leaden servitor to dull delay:** that is, timid speculation leads to dull delay.

60. **expedition:** speed.

62. **My counsel is my shield:** my shield is my only **counsel;** that is, there is no time for a conference on strategy.

And be inheritor of thy desire.
Farewell till then.

Tyr. I humbly take my leave. [*Exit.*]

Rich. The son of Clarence have I pent up close, 40
His daughter meanly have I matched in marriage,
The sons of Edward sleep in Abraham's bosom,
And Anne my wife hath bid this world good night.
Now, for I know the Britain Richmond aims
At young Elizabeth, my brother's daughter, 45
And by that knot looks proudly on the crown,
To her go I, a jolly thriving wooer.

Enter *Ratcliffe.*

Rat. My lord—

Rich. Good or bad news, that thou comest in so bluntly? 50

Rat. Bad news, my lord. Morton is fled to Richmond,
And Buckingham, backed with the hardy Welshmen,
Is in the field, and still his power increaseth.

Rich. Ely with Richmond troubles me more near 55
Than Buckingham and his rash-levied strength.
Come! I have learned that fearful commenting
Is leaden servitor to dull delay;
Delay leads impotent and snail-paced beggary.
Then fiery expedition be my wing, 60
Jove's Mercury, and herald for a king!
Go, muster men. My counsel is my shield;
We must be brief when traitors brave the field.

Exeunt.

IV. [iv.] The Duchess of York and Queen Elizabeth lament the death of the princes and curse Richard for his bloody deeds. Margaret of Anjou taunts them and rejoices that their troubles equal those she herself has known. Richard himself appears at the head of his army and takes the opportunity of telling Queen Elizabeth of his devoted love for her daughter. His honeyed words apparently dispel her bitterness, and she promises to inform her daughter of the King's wish to marry her.

News comes of rebellion throughout the land. Richmond, after a storm at sea, has finally landed, but Buckingham's army has been dispersed and he has been captured. Richard orders his army to march on to Salisbury and gives instructions for Buckingham to be brought to him there.

5. **induction:** introductory episode; see I. i. 32.

6. **consequence:** conclusion.

11. **unblown:** unopened; still in the bud; **new-appearing sweets:** young, fragrant flowers.

19. **crazed:** cracked.

Scene [IV. London. Before the Palace.]

Enter *Old Queen Margaret.*

Queen M. So now prosperity begins to mellow
And drop into the rotten mouth of death.
Here in these confines slily have I lurked
To watch the waning of mine enemies.
A dire induction am I witness to, 5
And will to France, hoping the consequence
Will prove as bitter, black, and tragical.
Withdraw thee, wretched Margaret! Who comes
here? [*Retires.*]

Enter *Duchess* [*of York*] and *Queen* [*Elizabeth*].

Queen. Ah, my poor princes! ah, my tender babes! 10
My unblown flowers, new-appearing sweets!
If yet your gentle souls fly in the air
And be not fixed in doom perpetual,
Hover about me with your airy wings
And hear your mother's lamentation! 15
Queen M. [*Aside*] Hover about her. Say that right
for right
Hath dimmed your infant morn to aged night.
Duch. So many miseries have crazed my voice
That my woe-wearied tongue is still and mute. 20
Edward Plantagenet, why art thou dead?

22. **quit:** pay for.

24. **dying debt:** i.e., the debt of death.

28. **When:** when before.

31. **mortal-living:** dead-alive.

33-4. **grave's due by life usurped:** that is, a corpse over which life improperly retains control.

43. **reverent:** entitled to respect.

44. **seniory:** seniority.

45. **frown on the upper hand:** be acknowledged the greater.

47. **Tell o'er:** review.

Queen M. [*Aside*] Plantagenet doth quit Plantagenet;
Edward for Edward pays a dying debt.

Queen. Wilt Thou, O God, fly from such gentle lambs 25
And throw them in the entrails of the wolf?
When didst Thou sleep when such a deed was done?

Queen M. [*Aside*] When holy Harry died, and my sweet son. 30

Duch. Dead life, blind sight, poor mortal-living ghost,
Woe's scene, world's shame, grave's due by life usurped,
Brief abstract and record of tedious days, 35
Rest thy unrest on England's lawful earth,
[*Sitting down.*]
Unlawfully made drunk with innocent blood!

Queen. Ah that thou wouldst as soon afford a grave
As thou canst yield a melancholy seat!
Then would I hide my bones, not rest them here. 40
Ah, who hath any cause to mourn but we?
[*Sitting down by her.*]

Queen M. [*Comes forward.*] If ancient sorrow be most reverent,
Give mine the benefit of seniory
And let my griefs frown on the upper hand. 45
If sorrow can admit society,
[*Sitting down with them.*]
Tell o'er your woes again by viewing mine.
I had an Edward, till a Richard killed him;
I had a Harry, till a Richard killed him:

52. **Richard:** i.e., her husband, the Duke of York.

53. **holpst:** helped; see I. ii. 119.

61. **reigns in galled eyes of weeping souls:** i.e., is supreme in being able to produce sore eyes in tearful victims.

62. **excellent grand:** surpassingly great.

65. **carnal:** carnivorous; flesh-eating.

71. **I cloy me:** I am being fully satisfied.

74. **boot:** an addition; an extra.

77. **frantic play:** violent act; i.e., that of Edward's murder.

78. **adulterate:** adulterous (because of his amour with Jane Shore).

80. **intelligencer:** agent or spy.

Thou hadst an Edward, till a Richard killed him; 50
Thou hadst a Richard, till a Richard killed him.
Duch. I had a Richard too, and thou didst kill him;
I had a Rutland too, thou holpst to kill him.
Queen M. Thou hadst a Clarence too, and Richard killed him. 55
From forth the kennel of thy womb hath crept
A hellhound that doth hunt us all to death:
That dog, that had his teeth before his eyes,
To worry lambs and lap their gentle blood,
That foul defacer of God's handiwork, 60
That reigns in galled eyes of weeping souls,
That excellent grand tyrant of the earth,
Thy womb let loose to chase us to our graves.
O upright, just, and true-disposing God,
How do I thank Thee that this carnal cur 65
Preys on the issue of his mother's body
And makes her pew-fellow with others' moan!
Duch. O Harry's wife, triumph not in my woes!
God witness with me, I have wept for thine.
Queen M. Bear with me! I am hungry for revenge, 70
And now I cloy me with beholding it.
Thy Edward he is dead, that killed my Edward;
Thy other Edward dead, to quit my Edward;
Young York he is but boot, because both they
Matched not the high perfection of my loss. 75
Thy Clarence he is dead that stabbed my Edward,
And the beholders of this frantic play,
The adulterate Hastings, Rivers, Vaughan, Grey,
Untimely smothered in their dusky graves.
Richard yet lives, hell's black intelligencer; 80

81. **Only reserved their factor:** retained only as their agent.

96. **index:** prologue; see II. ii. 162; **pageant:** spectacle.

99. **garish flag:** colored banner.

102. **in jest, only to fill the scene:** i.e., a player-queen acting only as an extra, with no dialogue or action.

109. **Decline:** recite or review in order.

Only reserved their factor to buy souls
And send them thither. But at hand, at hand,
Ensues his piteous and unpitied end.
Earth gapes, hell burns, fiends roar, saints pray,
To have him suddenly conveyed from hence. 85
Cancel his bond of life, dear God, I pray,
That I may live and say, "The dog is dead."

Queen. O, thou didst prophesy the time would come
That I should wish for thee to help me curse 90
That bottled spider, that foul bunch-backed toad!

Queen M. I called thee then vain flourish of my fortune;
I called thee then poor shadow, painted queen;
The presentation of but what I was, 95
The flattering index of a direful pageant;
One heaved a-high to be hurled down below;
A mother only mocked with two fair babes;
A dream of what thou wast, a garish flag,
To be the aim of every dangerous shot; 100
A sign of dignity, a breath, a bubble;
A queen in jest, only to fill the scene.
Where is thy husband now? Where be thy brothers?
Where be thy two sons? Wherein dost thou joy?
Who sues and kneels and says, "God save the Queen"? 105
Where be the bending peers that flattered thee?
Where be the thronging troops that followed thee?
Decline all this, and see what now thou art:
For happy wife, a most distressed widow; 110
For joyful mother, one that wails the name;

113. **caitiff:** wretch.

117-18. **the course of justice whirled about/ And left thee but a very prey to time:** i.e., the wheel of Fortune has turned and you are a mere prey to the ills of these times.

122. **proportion:** degree.

136. **Revolving:** thinking of; contemplating; see IV. ii. 47.

137. **quicken:** sharpen.

For one being sued to, one that humbly sues;
For Queen, a very caitiff crowned with care;
For she that scorned at me, now scorned of me;
For she being feared of all, now fearing one; 115
For she commanding all, obeyed of none.
Thus hath the course of justice whirled about
And left thee but a very prey to time,
Having no more but thought of what thou wast,
To torture thee the more, being what thou art. 120
Thou didst usurp my place, and dost thou not
Usurp the just proportion of my sorrow?
Now thy proud neck bears half my burdened yoke,
From which even here I slip my weary head
And leave the burden of it all on thee. 125
Farewell, York's wife, and queen of sad mischance!
These English woes shall make me smile in France.

Queen. O thou well skilled in curses, stay awhile,
And teach me how to curse mine enemies!

Queen M. Forbear to sleep the nights, and fast the days; 130
Compare dead happiness with living woe;
Think that thy babes were sweeter than they were,
And he that slew them fouler than he is:
Bett'ring thy loss makes the bad causer worse; 135
Revolving this will teach thee how to curse.

Queen. My words are dull. O quicken them with thine!

Queen M. Thy woes will make them sharp and pierce like mine. *Exit [Queen] Margaret.* 140

Duch. Why should calamity be full of words?

Queen. Windy attorneys to their client's woes,

143. **succeeders of intestate joys:** heirs of joys that died leaving no will.

151. **expedition:** both "haste" and "military errand" are probably meant.

158. **owed:** owned.

166. **flourish:** a series of notes.

168. **Rail on:** exclaim against.

Airy succeeders of intestate joys,
Poor breathing orators of miseries,
Let them have scope! Though what they will impart 145
Help nothing else, yet do they ease the heart.

Duch. If so, then be not tongue-tied: go with me,
And in the breath of bitter words let's smother
My damned son that thy two sweet sons smothered.
The trumpet sounds. Be copious in exclaims. 150

Enter *King Richard* and his *Train*, marching, with Drums and Trumpets.

Rich. Who intercepts me in my expedition?

Duch. O, she that might have intercepted thee,
By strangling thee in her accursed womb,
From all the slaughters, wretch, that thou hast done!

Queen. Hidest thou that forehead with a golden crown 155
Where't should be branded, if that right were right,
The slaughter of the prince that owed that crown
And the dire death of my poor sons and brothers?
Tell me, thou villain-slave, where are my children? 160

Duch. Thou toad, thou toad, where is thy brother Clarence?
And little Ned Plantagenet, his son?

Queen. Where is the gentle Rivers, Vaughan, Grey?

Duch. Where is kind Hastings? 165

Rich. A flourish, trumpets! Strike alarum, drums!
Let not the heavens hear these telltale women
Rail on the Lord's anointed. Strike, I say!

Flourish. Alarums.

175. **condition:** temperament.

176. **accent:** language.

181. **stayed:** waited; i.e., at his birth.

187. **Tetchy:** irritable.

188. **frightful:** i.e., full of frights.

190. **age confirmed:** coming of age; maturity.

191. **kind in hatred:** masking your hatred by kind behavior.

194. **Humphrey Hour:** i.e., never. "To dine with Duke Humphrey" was a phrase meaning to go without dinner, deriving from the fashion of indigent Elizabethan gallants of walking in St. Paul's Cathedral near a monument, erroneously believed to be that of Duke Humphrey, instead of going to dinner. **Humphrey Hour** might therefore be the dinnerless dinner hour. The editor George Steevens suggested that this was a reference to some amour of the Duchess, but no one has been able to connect this possibility with the phrase.

197. **disgracious:** displeasing; see III. [vii.] 120.

Either be patient and entreat me fair,
Or with the clamorous report of war 170
Thus will I drown your exclamations.
Duch. Art thou my son?
Rich. Ay, I thank God, my father, and yourself.
Duch. Then patiently hear my impatience.
Rich. Madam, I have a touch of your condition, 175
That cannot brook the accent of reproof.
Duch. O let me speak!
Rich. Do then, but I'll not hear.
Duch. I will be mild and gentle in my words.
Rich. And brief, good mother, for I am in haste. 180
Duch. Art thou so hasty? I have stayed for thee,
God knows, in torment and in agony.
Rich. And came I not at last to comfort you?
Duch. No, by the Holy Rood, thou knowst it well,
Thou camest on earth to make the earth my hell. 185
A grievous burden was thy birth to me;
Tetchy and wayward was thy infancy;
Thy schooldays frightful, desp'rate, wild, and furious;
Thy prime of manhood daring, bold, and venturous;
Thy age confirmed, proud, subtle, sly, and bloody, 190
More mild, but yet more harmful—kind in hatred.
What comfortable hour canst thou name
That ever graced me with thy company?
Rich. Faith, none, but Humphrey Hour, that called your Grace 195
To breakfast once, forth of my company.
If I be so disgracious in your eye,
Let me march on and not offend you, madam.

224. **For:** as for.
226. **level:** take aim.

Strike up the drum.
Duch. I prithee hear me speak. 200
Rich. You speak too bitterly.
Duch. Hear me a word;
For I shall never speak to thee again.
Rich. So.
Duch. Either thou wilt die, by God's just ordinance, 205
Ere from this war thou turn a conqueror,
Or I with grief and extreme age shall perish
And never more behold thy face again.
Therefore take with thee my most grievous curse, 210
Which in the day of battle tire thee more
Than all the complete armor that thou wearst!
My prayers on the adverse party fight,
And there the little souls of Edward's children
Whisper the spirits of thine enemies 215
And promise them success and victory!
Bloody thou art, bloody will be thy end;
Shame serves thy life and doth thy death attend!
Exit.
Queen. Though far more cause, yet much less spirit to curse 220
Abides in me. I say amen to her.
Rich. Stay, madam; I must talk a word with you.
Queen. I have no more sons of the royal blood
For thee to slaughter. For my daughters, Richard,
They shall be praying nuns, not weeping queens; 225
And therefore level not to hit their lives.
Rich. You have a daughter called Elizabeth,

238. **only in that safety:** that is, for the very reason of their royal birth.

239. **opposite:** hostile.

241. **All unavoided:** completely unavoidable.

242. **avoided grace:** i.e., one who has denied grace; an evil person.

246. **cozened:** cheated.

248. **lanched:** lanced; pierced.

249. **all indirectly:** deviously.

253. **But that still use of grief:** that is, were it not that continual use of grief.

257. **reft:** bereft.

Virtuous and fair, royal and gracious.
Queen. And must she die for this? O let her live,
And I'll corrupt her manners, stain her beauty, 230
Slander myself as false to Edward's bed,
Throw over her the veil of infamy:
So she may live unscarred of bleeding slaughter,
I will confess she was not Edward's daughter.
Rich. Wrong not her birth; she is a royal princess. 235
Queen. To save her life, I'll say she is not so.
Rich. Her life is safest only in her birth.
Queen. And only in that safety died her brothers.
Rich. Lo, at their birth good stars were opposite.
Queen. No, to their lives ill friends were contrary. 240
Rich. All unavoided is the doom of destiny.
Queen. True, when avoided grace makes destiny:
My babes were destined to a fairer death,
If grace had blessed thee with a fairer life.
Rich. You speak as if that I had slain my cousins! 245
Queen. Cousins indeed, and by their uncle cozened
Of comfort, kingdom, kindred, freedom, life.
Whose hand soever lanched their tender hearts,
Thy head, all indirectly, gave direction.
No doubt the murd'rous knife was dull and blunt, 250
Till it was whetted on thy stone-hard heart
To revel in the entrails of my lambs.
But that still use of grief makes wild grief tame,
My tongue should to thy ears not name my boys
Till that my nails were anchored in thine eyes; 255
And I, in such a desp'rate bay of death,
Like a poor bark, of sails and tackling reft,

260. **success:** termination; result.

263-65. **What good is covered with the face of heaven,/ To be discovered:** what good may yet be revealed on earth.

271. **imperial type:** symbol of sovereignty.

274. **demise:** convey or transmit.

276. **withal endow a child of thine:** endow a child of thine with.

277. **So:** provided that; **Lethe:** a river in the nether regions, the waters of which induced forgetfulness.

280. **process:** story; see IV. [iii.] 35.

Rush all to pieces on thy rocky bosom.
Rich. Madam, so thrive I in my enterprise,
And dangerous success of bloody wars, 260
As I intend more good to you and yours
Than ever you or yours by me were harmed!
Queen. What good is covered with the face of heaven,
To be discovered, that can do me good? 265
Rich. The advancement of your children, gentle lady.
Queen. Up to some scaffold, there to lose their heads!
Rich. Unto the dignity and height of fortune, 270
The high imperial type of this earth's glory.
Queen. Flatter my sorrow with report of it:
Tell me, what state, what dignity, what honor
Canst thou demise to any child of mine?
Rich. Even all I have—ay, and myself and all— 275
Will I withal endow a child of thine,
So in the Lethe of thy angry soul
Thou drown the sad remembrance of those wrongs
Which thou supposest I have done to thee.
Queen. Be brief, lest that the process of thy kindness 280
Last longer telling than thy kindness' date.
Rich. Then know that from my soul I love thy daughter.
Queen. My daughter's mother thinks it with her soul. 285
Rich. What do you think?

288-89. **from thy soul:** i.e., Richard's love is not close to his soul; it lacks sincerity.

303. **humor:** temperament.

310. **sometime:** once.

Queen. That thou dost love my daughter from thy soul.
So from thy soul's love didst thou love her brothers, 290
And from my heart's love I do thank thee for it.

Rich. Be not so hasty to confound my meaning:
I mean that with my soul I love thy daughter
And do intend to make her Queen of England.

Queen. Well then, who dost thou mean shall be her king? 295

Rich. Even he that makes her Queen. Who else should be?

Queen. What, thou?

Rich. Even so. How think you of it? 300

Queen. How canst thou woo her?

Rich. That would I learn of you,
As one being best acquainted with her humor.

Queen. And wilt thou learn of me?

Rich. Madam, with all my heart. 305

Queen. Send to her by the man that slew her brothers
A pair of bleeding hearts; thereon engrave
"Edward" and "York"; then haply will she weep:
Therefore present to her—as sometime Margaret 310
Did to thy father, steeped in Rutland's blood—
A handkerchief, which say to her did drain
The purple sap from her sweet brother's body,
And bid her wipe her weeping eyes withal.
If this inducement move her not to love, 315
Send her a letter of thy noble deeds:
Tell her thou madest away her uncle Clarence,

319. **Madest quick conveyance with:** quickly did away with.

330. **shall:** that is, cannot help doing so.

335. **quicken your increase:** revitalize the offspring of your blood.

340. **metal:** substance; flesh.

342. **of:** by; **bid:** the past tense of "abide": endured.

Her uncle Rivers; ay, and for her sake,
Madest quick conveyance with her good aunt Anne.
Rich. You mock me, madam; this is not the way 320
To win your daughter.
Queen. There is no other way,
Unless thou couldst put on some other shape,
And not be Richard that hath done all this.
Rich. Say that I did all this for love of her. 325
Queen. Nay, then indeed she cannot choose but hate thee,
Having bought love with such a bloody spoil.
Rich. Look, what is done cannot be now amended:
Men shall deal unadvisedly sometimes, 330
Which afterhours gives leisure to repent.
If I did take the kingdom from your sons,
To make amends I'll give it to your daughter;
If I have killed the issue of your womb,
To quicken your increase I will beget 335
Mine issue of your blood upon your daughter.
A grandam's name is little less in love
Than is the doting title of a mother;
They are as children but one step below,
Even of your metal, of your very blood, 340
Of all one pain, save for a night of groans
Endured of her for whom you bid like sorrow:
Your children were vexation to your youth,
But mine shall be a comfort to your age.
The loss you have is but a son being King, 345
And by that loss your daughter is made Queen.
I cannot make you what amends I would;

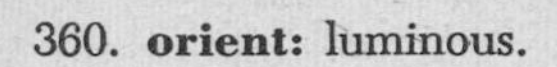

360. **orient:** luminous.

Therefore accept such kindness as I can.
Dorset your son, that with a fearful soul
Leads discontented steps in foreign soil, 350
This fair alliance quickly shall call home
To high promotions and great dignity.
The King, that calls your beauteous daughter wife,
Familiarly shall call thy Dorset brother:
Again shall you be mother to a king, 355
And all the ruins of distressful times
Repaired with double riches of content.
What! we have many goodly days to see:
The liquid drops of tears that you have shed
Shall come again, transformed to orient pearl, 360
Advantaging their love with interest
Of ten times double gain of happiness.
Go then, my mother; to thy daughter go;
Make bold her bashful years with your experience;
Prepare her ears to hear a wooer's tale; 365
Put in her tender heart the aspiring flame
Of golden sovereignty; acquaint the princess
With the sweet silent hours of marriage joys;
And when this arm of mine hath chastised
The petty rebel, dull-brained Buckingham, 370
Bound with triumphant garlands will I come
And lead thy daughter to a conqueror's bed;
To whom I will retail my conquest won,
And she shall be sole victress, Cæsar's Cæsar.

Queen. What were I best to say? Her father's brother 375
Would be her lord? Or shall I say her uncle?

382. **Infer:** suggest; see III. [v.] 80.

399-400. **sovereignty:** ruler; that is, such a ruler as Richard.

Or he that slew her brothers and her uncles?
Under what title shall I woo for thee
That God, the law, my honor, and her love 380
Can make seem pleasing to her tender years?

Rich. Infer fair England's peace by this alliance.

Queen. Which she shall purchase with still-lasting war.

Rich. Tell her the King, that may command, entreats. 385

Queen. That at her hands which the King's King forbids.

Rich. Say she shall be a high and mighty queen.

Queen. To wail the title, as her mother doth. 390

Rich. Say I will love her everlastingly.

Queen. But how long shall that title "ever" last?

Rich. Sweetly in force unto her fair life's end.

Queen. But how long fairly shall her sweet life last? 395

Rich. As long as heaven and nature lengthens it.

Queen. As long as hell and Richard likes of it.

Rich. Say I, her sovereign, am her subject low.

Queen. But she, your subject, loathes such sovereignty. 400

Rich. Be eloquent in my behalf to her.

Queen. An honest tale speeds best being plainly told.

Rich. Then plainly to her tell my loving tale.

Queen. Plain and not honest is too harsh a style. 405

Rich. Your reasons are too shallow and too quick.

Queen. O, no, my reasons are too deep and dead—

412. **George:** the pendant with the figure of St. George which formed part of the insignia of the Order of the Garter.

Drawing for the costume of Richard III as Duke of Gloucester. From a costume design by J. R. Planché (1829).

Too deep and dead, poor infants, in their graves.
Rich. Harp not on that string, madam; that is past.
Queen. Harp on it still shall I till heartstrings break. 410
Rich. Now, by my George, my garter, and my crown–
Queen. Profaned, dishonored, and the third usurped. 415
Rich. I swear–
Queen. By nothing, for this is no oath:
Thy George, profaned, hath lost his lordly honor;
Thy garter, blemished, pawned his knightly virtue;
Thy crown, usurped, disgraced his kingly glory. 420
If something thou wouldst swear to be believed,
Swear then by something that thou hast not wronged.
Rich. Then by myself–
Queen. Thyself is self-misused.
Rich. Now by the world– 425
Queen. 'Tis full of thy foul wrongs.
Rich. My father's death–
Queen. Thy life hath it dishonored.
Rich. Why then, by God–
Queen. God's wrong is most of all: 430
If thou didst fear to break an oath with Him,
The unity the King my husband made
Thou hadst not broken, nor my brothers died.
If thou hadst feared to break an oath by Him,
The imperial metal, circling now thy head, 435
Had graced the tender temples of my child,
And both the princes had been breathing here,
Which now, two tender bedfellows for dust,

455. **confound:** destroy.
461. **tender:** cherish; see I. i. 46 and II. iv. 83.

Thy broken faith hath made the prey for worms.
What canst thou swear by now? 440
Rich. The time to come.
Queen. That thou hast wronged in the time o'erpast;
For I myself have many tears to wash
Hereafter time, for time past wronged by thee. 445
The children live whose fathers thou hast slaughtered,
Ungoverned youth, to wail it in their age;
The parents live whose children thou hast butchered,
Old barren plants, to wail it with their age. 450
Swear not by time to come, for that thou hast
Misused ere used, by times ill-used o'erpast.
Rich. As I intend to prosper and repent,
So thrive I in my dangerous affairs
Of hostile arms! Myself myself confound! 455
Heaven and fortune bar me happy hours!
Day, yield me not thy light, nor, night, thy rest!
Be opposite all planets of good luck
To my proceeding if, with dear heart's love,
Immaculate devotion, holy thoughts, 460
I tender not thy beauteous princely daughter!
In her consists my happiness and thine;
Without her, follows to myself and thee,
Herself, the land, and many a Christian soul,
Death, desolation, ruin, and decay. 465
It cannot be avoided but by this;
It will not be avoided but by this.
Therefore, dear mother—I must call you so—
Be the attorney of my love to her:

473. **peevish-fond:** foolishly perverse.

476. **Shall I forget myself to be myself:** i.e., shall I forget who I am.

482. **recomforture:** comfort.

491. **puissant:** powerful.

492. **doubtful hollow-hearted friends:** friends of dubious loyalty.

Plead what I will be, not what I have been; 470
Not my deserts, but what I will deserve;
Urge the necessity and state of times,
And be not peevish-fond in great designs.

Queen. Shall I be tempted of the Devil thus?

Rich. Ay, if the Devil tempt you to do good. 475

Queen. Shall I forget myself to be myself?

Rich. Ay, if yourself's remembrance wrong yourself.

Queen. Yet thou didst kill my children.

Rich. But in your daughter's womb I bury them, 480
Where, in that nest of spicery, they will breed
Selves of themselves, to your recomforture.

Queen. Shall I go win my daughter to thy will?

Rich. And be a happy mother by the deed.

Queen. I go. Write to me very shortly, 485
And you shall understand from me her mind.

Rich. Bear her my true love's kiss; and so farewell—

Exit Q[ueen Elizabeth].

Relenting fool, and shallow, changing woman!

Enter *Ratcliffe*, [*Catesby* following].

How now? What news?

Rat. Most mighty sovereign, on the western coast 490
Rideth a puissant navy; to our shores
Throng many doubtful hollow-hearted friends,
Unarmed, and unresolved to beat them back.
'Tis thought that Richmond is their admiral;
And there they hull, expecting but the aid 495
Of Buckingham to welcome them ashore.

Archer and standard-bearer.
From a costume design by J. R. Planché (1829).

Rich. Some light-foot friend post to the Duke of Norfolk:
Ratcliffe, thyself—or Catesby—where is he?
Cates. Here, my good lord. 500
Rich. Catesby, fly to the Duke.
Cates. I will, my lord, with all convenient haste.
Rich. Ratcliffe, come hither. Post to Salisbury.
When thou comest thither—[*To Catesby*] Dull unmindful villain, 505
Why stayst thou here and goest not to the Duke?
Cates. First, mighty liege, tell me your Highness' pleasure,
What from your Grace I shall deliver to him.
Rich. O, true, good Catesby: bid him levy straight 510
The greatest strength and power that he can make
And meet me suddenly at Salisbury.
Cates. I go. *Exit.*
Rat. What, may it please you, shall I do at Salisbury? 515
Rich. Why, what wouldst thou do there before I go?
Rat. Your Highness told me I should post before.
Rich. My mind is changed.

Enter *Lord Stanley,* [*Earl of Derby*].

Stanley, what news with you? 520
Der. None good, my liege, to please you with the hearing,
Nor none so bad but well may be reported.

530. **runagate:** fugitive or vagabond, because after fleeing England for Brittany, he is now on the move again.

536. **the sword unswayed:** the royal sword of state unwielded.

Rich. Hoyday, a riddle! Neither good nor bad!
What needst thou run so many miles about, 525
When thou mayest tell thy tale the nearest way?
Once more, what news?
Der. Richmond is on the seas.
Rich. There let him sink, and be the seas on him!
White-livered runagate, what doth he there? 530
Der. I know not, mighty sovereign, but by guess.
Rich. Well, as you guess?
Der. Stirred up by Dorset, Buckingham, and Morton,
He makes for England, here to claim the crown. 535
Rich. Is the chair empty? is the sword unswayed?
Is the King dead? the empire unpossessed?
What heir of York is there alive but we?
And who is England's King but great York's heir?
Then tell me, what makes he upon the seas? 540
Der. Unless for that, my liege, I cannot guess.
Rich. Unless for that he comes to be your liege,
You cannot guess wherefore the Welshman comes.
Thou wilt revolt and fly to him, I fear.
Der. No, my good lord; therefore mistrust me not. 545
Rich. Where is thy power then to beat him back?
Where be thy tenants and thy followers?
Are they not now upon the western shore,
Safe-conducting the rebels from their ships?
Der. No, my good lord, my friends are in the North. 550
Rich. Cold friends to me! What do they in the North
When they should serve their sovereign in the West?

568. **his head's assurance:** i.e., the safety of his head.

572. **advertised:** informed.

575. **mo:** more.

578. **competitors:** associates.

A knight in complete armor.
From an 1883 reprint of *Caxton's Game and Playe of the Chesse* (1474).

Der. They have not been commanded, mighty King: 555
Pleaseth your Majesty to give me leave,
I'll muster up my friends and meet your Grace
Where and what time your Majesty shall please.

Rich. Ay, thou wouldst be gone to join with Richmond: 560
But I'll not trust thee.

Der. Most mighty sovereign,
You have no cause to hold my friendship doubtful.
I never was nor never will be false. 565

Rich. Go then and muster men. But leave behind
Your son, George Stanley. Look your heart be firm,
Or else his head's assurance is but frail.

Der. So deal with him as I prove true to you. *Exit.*

Enter a *Messenger.*

1. Mess. My gracious sovereign, now in Devonshire, 570
As I by friends am well advertised,
Sir Edward Courtney and the haughty prelate,
Bishop of Exeter, his elder brother,
With many mo confederates, are in arms. 575

Enter another *Messenger.*

2. Mess. In Kent, my liege, the Guildfords are in arms,
And every hour more competitors
Flock to the rebels, and their power grows strong.

581. **owls:** the owl's hoot was supposed to be an omen of death.

591. **well-advised:** judicious.

Enter another *Messenger*.

3. *Mess.* My lord, the army of great Buckingham— 580

Rich. Out on ye, owls! Nothing but songs of death? *He striketh him.*

There, take thou that, till thou bring better news.

3. *Mess.* The news I have to tell your Majesty
Is, that by sudden floods and fall of waters, 585
Buckingham's army is dispersed and scattered,
And he himself wand'red away alone,
No man knows whither.

Rich. I cry thee mercy:
There is my purse to cure that blow of thine. 590
Hath any well-advised friend proclaimed
Reward to him that brings the traitor in?

3. *Mess.* Such proclamation hath been made, my lord.

Enter another *Messenger*.

4. *Mess.* Sir Thomas Lovel and Lord Marquess Dorset, 595
'Tis said, my liege, in Yorkshire are in arms.
But this good comfort bring I to your Highness:
The Britain navy is dispersed by tempest;
Richmond in Dorsetshire sent out a boat 600
Unto the shore, to ask those on the banks
If they were his assistants, yea or no;
Who answered him they came from Buckingham

604. **Upon his party:** for his cause.
605. **Hoised:** hoisted; **Britain:** Brittany.

IV. [v.] Stanley sends a message to Richmond stating that because Richard holds his son as hostage, Stanley cannot openly send aid at present. He conveys the news, however, that the Queen has agreed to have her daughter Elizabeth marry Richmond. Stanley will lend assistance to Richmond's cause when he can safely do so.

---

1. **Sir:** Christopher Urswick held various ecclesiastical offices and is given the respectful title **Sir** on this account; see III. ii. 121.
3. **franked:** shut; see I. iii. 358.
6. **commend me:** tender my respectful greetings.

Upon his party. He, mistrusting them,
Hoised sail, and made his course again for Britain. 605
Rich. March on, march on, since we are up in arms;
If not to fight with foreign enemies,
Yet to beat down these rebels here at home.

Enter *Catesby.*

Cates. My liege, the Duke of Buckingham is taken.
That is the best news. That the Earl of Richmond 610
Is with a mighty power landed at Milford
Is colder tidings, but yet they must be told.
Rich. Away towards Salisbury! While we reason here,
A royal battle might be won and lost. 615
Someone take order Buckingham be brought
To Salisbury; the rest march on with me.
Flourish. Exeunt.

Scene [V. The Earl of Derby's house.]

Enter [*Lord Stanley, Earl of*] *Derby,* and *Sir Christopher* [*Urswick*].

Der. Sir Christopher, tell Richmond this from me:
That in the sty of the most deadly boar
My son George Stanley is franked up in hold;
If I revolt, off goes young George's head;
The fear of that holds off my present aid. 5
So get thee gone; commend me to thy lord.

10. **Pembroke:** the seat of Richmond's uncle, Jasper Tudor; **Ha'rford-West:** Haverford-West.

14. **redoubted:** formidable; dreaded; **Pembroke:** Jasper Tudor.

Withal say that the Queen hath heartily consented
He should espouse Elizabeth her daughter.
But tell me, where is princely Richmond now?
Chris. At Pembroke, or at Ha'rford-West in Wales. 10
Der. What men of name resort to him?
Chris. Sir Walter Herbert, a renowned soldier,
Sir Gilbert Talbot, Sir William Stanley,
Oxford, redoubted Pembroke, Sir James Blunt,
And Rice ap Thomas, with a valiant crew, 15
And many other of great name and worth;
And towards London do they bend their power,
If by the way they be not fought withal.
Der. Well, hie thee to thy lord. I kiss his hand:
My letter will resolve him of my mind. [*Gives letter.*] 20
Farewell.

Exeunt.

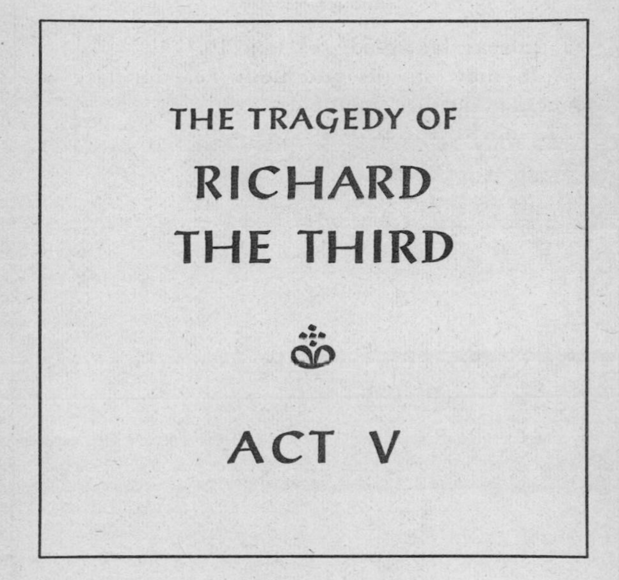

THE TRAGEDY OF

RICHARD THE THIRD

ACT V

V. i. Buckingham is brought forth to be executed. Richard has refused to speak with him, and Buckingham resignedly accepts his fate as a just judgment for his disloyalty to the family of Edward IV.

7. **miscarried:** died; see I. iii. 19.

9. **If that:** if; **discontented:** i.e., for lack of vengeance on their murderers.

11. **mock:** jeer at.

ACT V

Scene I. [Salisbury.]

Enter *Buckingham* with [the *Sheriff* and] *Halberds,* led to execution.

Buck. Will not King Richard let me speak with him?
Sher. No, my good lord; therefore be patient.
Buck. Hastings, and Edward's children, Grey and Rivers, 5
Holy King Henry and thy fair son Edward,
Vaughan, and all that have miscarried
By underhand corrupted foul injustice,
If that your moody discontented souls
Do through the clouds behold this present hour, 10
Even for revenge mock my destruction!
This is All Souls' day, fellow, is it not?
Sher. It is.
Buck. Why, then All Souls' day is my body's doomsday. 15
This is the day which, in King Edward's time,
I wished might fall on me when I was found
False to his children and his wife's allies;
This is the day wherein I wished to fall
By the false faith of him whom most I trusted; 20

22. **determined respite of my wrongs:** predetermined limit of my period of wrongdoing.

24. **feigned:** insincere; see II. i. 23.

V. ii. Richmond appears for the first time, leading his men toward an encounter with King Richard. The righteousness of his cause inspires him with confidence of success.

---

6. **father:** i.e., stepfather; see IV. ii. 95 note.

This, this All Souls' day to my fearful soul
Is the determined respite of my wrongs:
That high All-Seer which I dallied with
Hath turned my feigned prayer on my head
And given in earnest what I begged in jest. 25
Thus doth He force the swords of wicked men
To turn their own points in their masters' bosoms;
Thus Margaret's curse falls heavy on my neck:
"When he," quoth she, "shall split thy heart with sorrow, 30
Remember Margaret was a prophetess."
Come lead me, officers, to the block of shame.
Wrong hath but wrong, and blame the due of blame.

Exeunt Buckingham with Officers.

Scene II. [Tamworth. The camp of Richmond.]

Enter *Richmond, Oxford,* [*Sir James*] *Blunt,* [*Sir Walter*] *Herbert,* and others, with Drum and Colors.

Richm. Fellows in arms, and my most loving friends,
Bruised underneath the yoke of tyranny,
Thus far into the bowels of the land
Have we marched on without impediment; 5
And here receive we from our father Stanley
Lines of fair comfort and encouragement.
The wretched, bloody, and usurping boar,
That spoiled your summer fields and fruitful vines,

19. **Every man's conscience is a thousand men:** i.e., each man's certainty of being on the right side is worth a thousand men helping him fight.

V. [iii.] Richard and Richmond both encamp on Bosworth Field. When they sleep, the ghosts of Richard's murdered victims appear to each in his dreams, urging Richard to despair and die for the crimes he has committed, and promising victory to Richmond. Richard wakens with fearful recollections of the night's apparitions, but Richmond is heartened by the good omen of his dreams. Both exhort their men to fight valiantly. Richmond asserts the righteousness of his cause in seeking to overthrow a bloody usurper, while Richard describes his enemies as vagabonds and foreign upstarts.

Swills your warm blood like wash, and makes his trough 10
In your embowelled bosoms—this foul swine
Is now even in the center of this isle,
Near to the town of Leicester, as we learn:
From Tamworth thither is but one day's march. 15
In God's name cheerly on, courageous friends,
To reap the harvest of perpetual peace
By this one bloody trial of sharp war.

Ox. Every man's conscience is a thousand men,
To fight against this guilty homicide. 20

Her. I doubt not but his friends will turn to us.

Blunt. He hath no friends but what are friends for fear,
Which in his dearest need will fly from him.

Richm. All for our vantage. Then in God's name march! 25
True hope is swift and flies with swallow's wings;
Kings it makes gods, and meaner creatures kings.

Exeunt omnes.

[Scene III. Bosworth Field.]

Enter *King Richard* in arms, with *Norfolk, Ratcliffe,* and the *Earl of Surrey,* [and *Soldiers*].

Rich. Here pitch our tent, even here in Bosworth field.
My Lord of Surrey, why look you so sad?

7. **knocks:** buffets in battle.

11. **all's one for that:** that doesn't matter.

14. **battalia:** organized troops.

18. **the vantage of the ground:** where tactical advantage lies on the battle site.

19. **sound direction:** competent leadership.

23. **tract:** track; **his fiery car:** i.e., the chariot of the sun god.

28. **several:** respective.

John Howard, Duke of Norfolk.
From a costume design by J. R. Planché (1829).

Sur. My heart is ten times lighter than my looks.
Rich. My Lord of Norfolk— 5
Nor. Here, most gracious liege.
Rich. Norfolk, we must have knocks. Ha! must we not?
Nor. We must both give and take, my loving lord.
Rich. Up with my tent! Here will I lie tonight; 10
[*Soldiers begin to set up the King's tent.*]
But where tomorrow? Well, all's one for that.
Who hath descried the number of the traitors?
Nor. Six or seven thousand is their utmost power.
Rich. Why, our battalia trebles that account:
Besides, the King's name is a tower of strength, 15
Which they upon the adverse faction want.
Up with the tent! Come, noble gentlemen,
Let us survey the vantage of the ground.
Call for some men of sound direction:
Let's lack no discipline, make no delay, 20
For, lords, tomorrow is a busy day. *Exeunt.*

Enter *Richmond, Sir William Brandon, Oxford,* and *Dorset,* [*Herbert,* and *Blunt.* Some of the *Soldiers* pitch *Richmond's* tent.]

Richm. The weary sun hath made a golden set,
And by the bright tract of his fiery car
Gives token of a goodly day tomorrow.
Sir William Brandon, you shall bear my standard. 25
Give me some ink and paper in my tent:
I'll draw the form and model of our battle,
Limit each leader to his several charge,

32. **keeps:** i.e., stays with.

And part in just proportion our small power.
My Lord of Oxford, you, Sir William Brandon, 30
And you, Sir Walter Herbert, stay with me.
The Earl of Pembroke keeps his regiment;
Good Captain Blunt, bear my good night to him,
And by the second hour in the morning
Desire the Earl to see me in my tent: 35
Yet one thing more, good Captain, do for me—
Where is Lord Stanley quartered, do you know?

Blunt. Unless I have mista'en his colors much,
Which well I am assured I have not done,
His regiment lies half a mile at least 40
South from the mighty power of the King.

Richm. If without peril it be possible,
Sweet Blunt, make some good means to speak with him
And give him from me this most needful note. 45

Blunt. Upon my life, my lord, I'll undertake it;
And so God give you quiet rest tonight!

Richm. Good night, good Captain Blunt.

[*Exit Blunt.*]

Come, gentlemen,
Let us consult upon tomorrow's business. 50
Into my tent; the dew is raw and cold.

They withdraw into the tent.

Enter, [to his tent, *King*] *Richard, Ratcliffe, Norfolk,* and *Catesby.*

Rich. What is't o'clock?

Cates. It's suppertime, my lord;

57. **beaver:** visor of armored helmet.

72. **watch:** it is uncertain whether a guard or a watch light (by which the time could be told) is meant here.

74. **staves:** shafts of lances.

80. **cockshut time:** twilight.

It's nine o'clock.

Rich. I will not sup tonight. 55

Give me some ink and paper.

What, is my beaver easier than it was?

And all my armor laid into my tent?

Cates. It is, my liege; and all things are in readiness. 60

Rich. Good Norfolk, hie thee to thy charge;

Use careful watch, choose trusty sentinels.

Nor. I go, my lord.

Rich. Stir with the lark tomorrow, gentle Norfolk.

Nor. I warrant you, my lord. *Exit.* 65

Rich. Catesby!

Cates. My lord?

Rich. Send out a pursuivant-at-arms

To Stanley's regiment; bid him bring his power

Before sunrising, lest his son George fall 70

Into the blind cave of eternal night. [*Exit Catesby.*]

Fill me a bowl of wine. Give me a watch.

Saddle white Surrey for the field tomorrow.

Look that my staves be sound and not too heavy.

Ratcliffe! 75

Rat. My lord?

Rich. Sawst thou the melancholy Lord Northumberland?

Rat. Thomas the Earl of Surrey and himself,

Much about cockshut time, from troop to troop 80

Went through the army, cheering up the soldiers.

Rich. So, I am satisfied. Give me a bowl of wine.

I have not that alacrity of spirit

92. **father-in-law:** stepfather.

94. **attorney:** proxy.

97. **flaky:** still streaked with light.

99. **thy battle:** the troops under your command.

101. **mortal-staring:** deadly of glance; threatening death.

103. **With best advantage will deceive the time:** will fool Richard as best I can.

106. **tender George:** actually George Stanley, Lord Strange, was at this time a married adult.

Nor cheer of mind that I was wont to have.
[*Wine brought.*]
Set it down. Is ink and paper ready? 85
Rat. It is, my lord.
Rich. Bid my guard watch. Leave me.
Ratcliffe, about the mid of night come to my tent
And help to arm me. Leave me, I say.
Exit Ratcliffe.
[*King Richard withdraws into his tent.*]

Enter [*Lord Stanley, Earl of*] *Derby,* to *Richmond* in his tent, [*Lords* and others attending].

Der. Fortune and victory sit on thy helm! 90
Richm. All comfort that the dark night can afford
Be to thy person, noble father-in-law!
Tell me, how fares our loving mother?
Der. I, by attorney, bless thee from thy mother,
Who prays continually for Richmond's good: 95
So much for that. The silent hours steal on,
And flaky darkness breaks within the East.
In brief, for so the season bids us be,
Prepare thy battle early in the morning
And put thy fortune to the arbitrament 100
Of bloody strokes and mortal-staring war.
I, as I may—that which I would I cannot—
With best advantage will deceive the time
And aid thee in this doubtful shock of arms.
But on thy side I may not be too forward, 105
Lest, being seen, thy brother, tender George,

108. **leisure:** time allowed; free time.
113. **speed:** prosper.
116. **peise:** weigh.
121. **irons:** swords.
126. **watchful:** wakeful.

Be executed in his father's sight.
Farewell. The leisure and the fearful time
Cuts off the ceremonious vows of love
And ample interchange of sweet discourse 110
Which so-long-sund'red friends should dwell upon.
God give us leisure for these rites of love!
Once more adieu: be valiant, and speed well!

Richm. Good lords, conduct him to his regiment.
I'll strive with troubled noise to take a nap, 115
Lest leaden slumber peise me down tomorrow,
When I should mount with wings of victory:
Once more, good night, kind lords and gentlemen.

Exeunt. Manet Richmond.

O Thou, whose captain I account myself,
Look on my forces with a gracious eye; 120
Put in their hands Thy bruising irons of wrath,
That they may crush down with a heavy fall
The usurping helmets of our adversaries;
Make us Thy ministers of chastisement,
That we may praise Thee in the victory. 125
To Thee I do commend my watchful soul
Ere I let fall the windows of mine eyes:
Sleeping and waking, O defend me still! *Sleeps.*

Enter the *Ghost of Prince Edward,* son to *Henry the Sixth.*

Ghost. (*To Richard*) Let me sit heavy on thy soul tomorrow! 130
Think how thou stab'dst me in my prime of youth

148. **fulsome:** satiating.
151. **fall:** drop.

At Tewkesbury: despair therefore, and die!
(*To Richmond*) Be cheerful, Richmond; for the wronged souls
Of butchered princes fight in thy behalf. 135
King Henry's issue, Richmond, comforts thee.

Enter the *Ghost of Henry the Sixth.*

Ghost. [*To Richard*] When I was mortal, my anointed body
By thee was punched full of deadly holes.
Think on the Tower and me: despair, and die! 140
Harry the Sixth bids thee despair, and die!
(*To Richmond*) Virtuous and holy, be thou conqueror!
Harry, that prophesied thou shouldst be King,
Doth comfort thee in thy sleep: live, and flourish! 145

Enter the *Ghost of Clarence.*

Ghost. [*To Richard*] Let me sit heavy in thy soul tomorrow—
I, that was washed to death with fulsome wine,
Poor Clarence by thy guile betrayed to death!
Tomorrow in the battle think on me, 150
And fall thy edgeless sword: despair, and die!
(*To Richmond*) Thou offspring of the house of Lancaster,
The wronged heirs of York do pray for thee;
Good angels guard thy battle! Live, and flourish! 155

St. George slaying the dragon.
From Agostino Giustiniani, *Castigatissimi annali* (1537).
(See V. [iii.] 390-91.)

Enter the *Ghosts of Rivers, Grey,* and *Vaughan.*

Riv. [*To Richard*] Let me sit heavy in thy soul to-morrow,
Rivers, that died at Pomfret! Despair, and die!
Grey. Think upon Grey, and let thy soul despair!
Vaugh. Think upon Vaughan, and with guilty fear 160
Let fall thy lance: despair, and die!
All. (*To Richmond*) Awake, and think our wrongs in Richard's bosom
Will conquer him! Awake, and win the day!

Enter the *Ghost of Lord Hastings.*

Ghost. [*To Richard*] Bloody and guilty, guiltily awake 165
And in a bloody battle end thy days!
Think on Lord Hastings: despair, and die!
(*To Richmond*) Quiet untroubled soul, awake, awake! 170
Arm, fight, and conquer, for fair England's sake!

Enter the *Ghosts of the two young Princes.*

Ghosts. [*To Richard*] Dream on thy cousins smothered in the Tower.
Let us be lead within thy bosom, Richard,
And weigh thee down to ruin, shame and death! 175
Thy nephews' souls bid thee despair, and die!

179. **annoy:** harm (from the boar).
199. **for hope:** i.e., because of planning to help.

(*To Richmond*) Sleep, Richmond, sleep in peace and wake in joy.
Good angels guard thee from the boar's annoy!
Live, and beget a happy race of kings! 180
Edward's unhappy sons do bid thee flourish.

Enter the *Ghost of Anne*, his wife.

Ghost. (*To Richard*) Richard, thy wife, that wretched Anne thy wife,
That never slept a quiet hour with thee,
Now fills thy sleep with perturbations: 185
Tomorrow in the battle think on me,
And fall thy edgeless sword: despair, and die!
(*To Richmond*) Thou quiet soul, sleep thou a quiet sleep.
Dream of success and happy victory! 190
Thy adversary's wife doth pray for thee.

Enter the *Ghost of Buckingham*.

Ghost. (*To Richard*) The first was I that helped thee to the crown;
The last was I that felt thy tyranny.
O, in the battle think on Buckingham, 195
And die in terror of thy guiltiness!
Dream on, dream on, of bloody deeds and death:
Fainting, despair; despairing, yield thy breath!
(*To Richmond*) I died for hope ere I could lend thee aid; 200
But cheer thy heart and be thou not dismayed:

225. **All several sins, all used in each degree:** every different sin, every one committed to the utmost degree.

God and good angels fight on Richmond's side,
And Richard fall in height of all his pride!

[The Ghosts vanish.] Richard starts out of his dream.

Rich. Give me another horse! Bind up my wounds!
Have mercy, Jesu! Soft! I did but dream. 205
O coward conscience, how dost thou afflict me!
The lights burn blue. It is now dead midnight.
Cold fearful drops stand on my trembling flesh.
What do I fear? Myself? There's none else by.
Richard loves Richard: that is, I am I. 210
Is there a murderer here? No. Yes, I am:
Then fly. What, from myself? Great reason why:
Lest I revenge. What, myself upon myself?
Alack, I love myself. Wherefore? For any good
That I myself have done unto myself? 215
O, no! Alas, I rather hate myself
For hateful deeds committed by myself.
I am a villain. Yet I lie, I am not.
Fool, of thyself speak well. Fool, do not flatter.
My conscience hath a thousand several tongues, 220
And every tongue brings in a several tale,
And every tale condemns me for a villain.
Perjury, perjury, in the highest degree;
Murder, stern murder, in the direst degree;
All several sins, all used in each degree, 225
Throng to the bar, crying all, "Guilty! guilty!"
I shall despair. There is no creature loves me;
And if I die, no soul shall pity me.

248. **proof:** stout armor.
253. **Cry mercy:** I beg your pardon.

Nay, wherefore should they, since that I myself
Find in myself no pity to myself? 230
Methought the souls of all that I had murdered
Came to my tent, and every one did threat
Tomorrow's vengeance on the head of Richard.

Enter *Ratcliffe*.

Rat. My lord!
Rich. Who's there? 235
Rat. Ratcliffe, my lord, 'tis I. The early village cock
Hath twice done salutation to the morn:
Your friends are up and buckle on their armor.
Rich. O Ratcliffe, I have dreamed a fearful dream! 240
What thinkst thou? Will our friends prove all true?
Rat. No doubt, my lord.
Rich. O Ratcliffe, I fear, I fear!
Rat. Nay, good my lord, be not afraid of shadows.
Rich. By the apostle Paul, shadows tonight 245
Have struck more terror to the soul of Richard
Than can the substance of ten thousand soldiers
Armed in proof and led by shallow Richmond.
'Tis not yet near day. Come, go with me.
Under our tents I'll play the eavesdropper, 250
To hear if any mean to shrink from me.
Exeunt Richard and Ratcliffe.

Enter the *Lords* to *Richmond* sitting in his tent.

Lords. Good morrow, Richmond.
Richm. Cry mercy, lords and watchful gentlemen,
That you have ta'en a tardy sluggard here.

262. **cried on:** invoked.

270. **leisure:** i.e., lack of it; see l. 108.

275. **except:** excepted.

278. **tyrant:** usurper.

279. **One raised in blood and one in blood established:** one who elevated himself to his high position and has maintained himself there by bloody deeds.

280. **made means to come by what he hath:** i.e., took matters into his own hands to achieve his ambition instead of becoming King by lawful succession.

Lords. How have you slept, my lord? 255
Richm. The sweetest sleep, and fairest-boding dreams
That ever ent'red in a drowsy head
Have I since your departure had, my lords.
Methought their souls whose bodies Richard murdered 260
Came to my tent and cried on victory.
I promise you my heart is very jocund
In the remembrance of so fair a dream.
How far into the morning is it, lords? 265
Lords. Upon the stroke of four.
Richm. Why, then 'tis time to arm and give direction.

His Oration to his Soldiers.

More than I have said, loving countrymen,
The leisure and enforcement of the time 270
Forbids to dwell upon. Yet remember this:
God and our good cause fight upon our side;
The prayers of holy saints and wronged souls,
Like high-reared bulwarks, stand before our faces.
Richard except, those whom we fight against 275
Had rather have us win than him they follow.
For what is he they follow? Truly, gentlemen,
A bloody tyrant and a homicide;
One raised in blood and one in blood established;
One that made means to come by what he hath, 280
And slaughtered those that were the means to help him;

283-84. **A base foul stone, made precious by the foil/ Of England's chair:** one of common substance who appears glorious because of the dignity lent him by the English throne.

287. **ward:** guard.

291. **Your country's fat shall pay your pains the hire:** that is, the wages for your efforts will be paid from your country's abundance.

295. **quits it in your age:** will repay you when you are old. **Quits** equals "requites."

297. **Advance:** raise; see I. ii. 42.

298-99. **the ransom of my bold attempt/ Shall be this cold corpse:** i.e., I will not sue for ransom if the battle should go against us, but will fight to the death.

A base foul stone, made precious by the foil
Of England's chair, where he is falsely set;
One that hath ever been God's enemy. 285
Then if you fight against God's enemy,
God will in justice ward you as his soldiers;
If you do sweat to put a tyrant down,
You sleep in peace, the tyrant being slain;
If you do fight against your country's foes, 290
Your country's fat shall pay your pains the hire;
If you do fight in safeguard of your wives,
Your wives shall welcome home the conquerors;
If you do free your children from the sword,
Your children's children quits it in your age: 295
Then in the name of God and all these rights,
Advance your standards, draw your willing swords.
For me, the ransom of my bold attempt
Shall be this cold corpse on the earth's cold face;
But if I thrive, the gain of my attempt 300
The least of you shall share his part thereof.
Sound drums and trumpets boldly and cheerfully:
God and Saint George! Richmond and victory!
[*Exeunt.*]

Enter *King Richard, Ratcliffe,* [and *Soldiers*].

Rich. What said Northumberland as touching Richmond? 305
Rat. That he was never trained up in arms.
Rich. He said the truth. And what said Surrey then?

312. **Tell:** i.e., count its strokes.

325. **sadly:** soberly.

326. **vaunts in the field:** i.e., is in the field before us.

327. **Caparison:** deck in trappings.

King Richard armed.
From a costume design by J. R. Planché (1829).

Rat. He smiled and said, "The better for our purpose." 310

Rich. He was in the right, and so indeed it is.

Clock strikes.

Tell the clock there. Give me a calendar.
Who saw the sun today?

Rat. Not I, my lord.

Rich. Then he disdains to shine; for by the book 315
He should have braved the East an hour ago.
A black day will it be to somebody.
Ratcliffe!

Rat. My lord?

Rich. The sun will not be seen today; 320
The sky doth frown and lower upon our army.
I would these dewy tears were from the ground.
Not shine today? Why, what is that to me
More than to Richmond? For the selfsame heaven
That frowns on me looks sadly upon him. 325

Enter *Norfolk.*

Nor. Arm, arm, my lord; the foe vaunts in the field.

Rich. Come, bustle, bustle! Caparison my horse!
Call up Lord Stanley, bid him bring his power.
I will lead forth my soldiers to the plain,
And thus my battle shall be ordered: 330
My foreward shall be drawn out all in length,
Consisting equally of horse and foot;
Our archers shall be placed in the midst;
John Duke of Norfolk, Thomas Earl of Surrey,

339. **to boot:** in addition; see IV. [iv.] 74.
343. **Jockey:** a nickname for the name John.
344. **Dickon:** a nickname for the name Richard.
353. **inferred:** mentioned; see III. [v.] 80 and IV. [iv.] 382.
354. **cope withal:** encounter.
355. **sort:** company.
356. **Britains:** Bretons.

Shall have the leading of this foot and horse. 335
They thus directed, we will follow
In the main battle, whose puissance on either side
Shall be well winged with our chiefest horse.
This, and Saint George to boot! What thinkst thou,
Norfolk? 340

Nor. A good direction, warlike sovereign.
This found I on my tent this morning.

He showeth him a paper.

"Jockey of Norfolk, be not so bold,
For Dickon thy master is bought and sold."

Rich. A thing devised by the enemy. 345
Go, gentlemen, every man to his charge.
Let not our babbling dreams affright our souls;
Conscience is but a word that cowards use,
Devised at first to keep the strong in awe:
Our strong arms be our conscience, swords our law! 350
March on, join bravely, let us to't pell-mell,
If not to heaven, then hand in hand to hell.

His Oration to his Army.

What shall I say more than I have inferred?
Remember whom you are to cope withal:
A sort of vagabonds, rascals, and runaways, 355
A scum of Britains and base lackey peasants,
Whom their o'ercloyed country vomits forth
To desperate adventures and assured destruction.
You sleeping safe, they bring to you unrest;
You having lands, and blessed with beauteous wives, 360

361. **distain:** stain with dishonor.

363. **at our mother's cost:** this is an error picked up from the second edition of Holinshed's *Chronicles,* which reads: "brought vp by my moothers meanes, and mine, like a captiue in a close cage, in the court of Francis duke of Britaine . . ." Hall's earlier history reads "brother" and Holinshed did likewise in his first edition. What was probably meant by the phrase was only that Richmond's residence at the court of the Duke of Britaine was due to fear of Edward IV and Richard; he was not maintained there at their expense.

369. **fond:** foolish; see III. iv. 85; IV. [iv.] 473.

373. **bobbed:** buffeted.

379. **to the head:** that is, as far back as your bowstrings will go.

381. **Amaze the welkin:** terrify the heavens.

They would restrain the one, distain the other.
And who doth lead them but a paltry fellow,
Long kept in Britain at our mother's cost,
A milksop, one that never in his life
Felt so much cold as over shoes in snow? 365
Let's whip these stragglers o'er the seas again,
Lash hence these overweening rags of France,
These famished beggars, weary of their lives,
Who, but for dreaming on this fond exploit,
For want of means, poor rats, had hanged themselves. 370
If we be conquered, let men conquer us,
And not these bastard Britains, whom our fathers
Have in their own land beaten, bobbed, and thumped,
And, in record, left them the heirs of shame.
Shall these enjoy our lands? lie with our wives? 375
Ravish our daughters? (*Drum afar off.*) Hark! I hear
their drum.
Fight, gentlemen of England! Fight, bold yeomen!
Draw, archers, draw your arrows to the head!
Spur your proud horses hard, and ride in blood! 380
Amaze the welkin with your broken staves!

Enter a *Messenger.*

What says Lord Stanley? Will he bring his power?
Mess. My lord, he doth deny to come.
Rich. Off with his son George's head!
Nor. My lord, the enemy is past the marsh: 385
After the battle let George Stanley die.
Rich. A thousand hearts are great within my
bosom!

390. **word:** motto; symbol.

391. **spleen:** violent rage. Anger was believed to derive from the **spleen;** see II. iv. 73.

V. [iv.] King Richard is fighting savagely afoot, having lost his horse. He has sought vainly to engage Richmond in single combat in order to settle the conflict decisively.

Ent. **excursions:** clashes of arms.

3. **Daring an opposite to every danger:** challenging every danger to combat him.

9. **set:** wagered.

10. **die:** singular of dice.

Advance our standards, set upon our foes.
Our ancient word of courage, fair Saint George, 390
Inspire us with the spleen of fiery dragons!
Upon them! Victory sits on our helms.
[*Exeunt.*]

[Scene IV. Another part of the field.]

Alarum; excursions. Enter [*Norfolk* and *Forces;* to him] *Catesby.*

Cates. Rescue, my Lord of Norfolk, rescue, rescue!
The King enacts more wonders than a man,
Daring an opposite to every danger:
His horse is slain, and all on foot he fights,
Seeking for Richmond in the throat of death. 5
Rescue, fair lord, or else the day is lost!

Alarums. Enter [*King*] *Richard.*

Rich. A horse! a horse! my kingdom for a horse!
Cates. Withdraw, my lord; I'll help you to a horse.
Rich. Slave, I have set my life upon a cast,
And I will stand the hazard of the die. 10
I think there be six Richmonds in the field;
Five have I slain today instead of him.
A horse! a horse! my kingdom for a horse!
[*Exeunt.*]

V. [v.] King Richard fights Richmond and is killed. Richmond announces the victory and prophesies an end of the wars between the houses of Lancaster and York and long-lasting peace to come by his union with Elizabeth of York.

---

20. **we have ta'en the sacrament:** I have sworn.

[Scene V. Another part of the field.]

Alarum. Enter [*King*] *Richard* and *Richmond;* they fight; *Richard* is slain.

Retreat and flourish. Enter *Richmond,* [*Lord Stanley, Earl of*] *Derby,* bearing the crown, with divers other *Lords.*

Richm. God and your arms be praised, victorious friends!
The day is ours; the bloody dog is dead.
Der. Courageous Richmond, well hast thou acquit thee. 5
Lo, here this long usurped royalty
From the dead temples of this bloody wretch
Have I plucked off, to grace thy brows withal.
Wear it, enjoy it, and make much of it.
Richm. Great God of heaven, say amen to all! 10
But tell me, is young George Stanley living?
Der. He is, my lord, and safe in Leicester town,
Whither, if it please you, we may now withdraw us.
Richm. What men of name are slain on either side?
Der. John Duke of Norfolk, Walter Lord Ferrers, 15
Sir Robert Brakenbury, and Sir William Brandon.
Richm. Inter their bodies as become their births.
Proclaim a pardon to the soldiers fled
That in submission will return to us;
And then, as we have ta'en the sacrament, 20
We will unite the White Rose and the Red.

22. **conjunction:** marriage.

37. **Abate the edge of traitors:** i.e., reduce their power to harm the kingdom.

38. **reduce:** lead back to; restore.

Smile heaven upon this fair conjunction,
That long have frowned upon their enmity!
What traitor hears me, and says not amen?
England hath long been mad and scarred herself; 25
The brother blindly shed the brother's blood;
The father rashly slaughtered his own son;
The son, compelled, been butcher to the sire:
All this divided York and Lancaster,
Divided in their dire division, 30
O now let Richmond and Elizabeth,
The true succeeders of each royal house,
By God's fair ordinance conjoin together!
And let their heirs, God, if Thy will be so,
Enrich the time to come with smooth-faced peace, 35
With smiling plenty, and fair prosperous days!
Abate the edge of traitors, gracious Lord,
That would reduce these bloody days again
And make poor England weep in streams of blood!
Let them not live to taste this land's increase 40
That would with treason wound this fair land's peace!
Now civil wounds are stopped, peace lives again:
That she may long live here, God say amen!

Exeunt.

KEY TO

Famous Lines and Phrases

Now is the winter of our discontent
Made glorious summer by this sun of York.
[*Richard*–I. i. 1–2]

O wonderful, when devils tell the truth!
[*Anne*–I. ii. 76]

Was ever woman in this humor wooed?
Was ever woman in this humor won?
[*Richard*–I. ii. 258–59]

A sweeter and a lovelier gentleman
Framed in the prodigality of nature . . .
The spacious world cannot again afford. . . .
[*Richard*–I. ii. 274–77]

I do mistake my person all this while!
Upon my life, she finds, although I cannot,
Myself to be a marv'lous proper man.
I'll be at charges for a looking glass
And entertain a score or two of tailors. . . .
Shine out, fair sun, till I have bought a glass,
That I may see my shadow as I pass.
[*Richard*–I. ii. 284–95]

Cannot a plain man live and think no harm,
But thus his simple truth must be abused
With silken, sly, insinuating Jacks?
[*Richard*–I. iii. 61–3]

. . . the world is grown so bad
That wrens make prey where eagles dare not perch.
Since every Jack became a gentleman,
There's many a gentle person made a Jack.
[*Richard*–I. iii. 81–4]

The first that there did greet my stranger-soul
Was my great father-in-law, renowned Warwick,
Who spake aloud, "What scourge for perjury
Can this dark monarchy afford false Clarence?"
And so he vanished. Then came wand'ring by
A shadow like an angel, with bright hair
Dabbled in blood, and he shrieked out aloud,
"Clarence is come—false, fleeting, perjured Clarence,
That stabbed me in the field by Tewkesbury. . . ."

[*Clarence*—I. iv. 50–8]

O momentary grace of mortal men,
Which we more hunt for than the grace of God!
Who builds his hope in air of your good looks
Lives like a drunken sailor on a mast,
Ready with every nod to tumble down
Into the fatal bowels of the deep.

[*Hastings*—III. iv. 101–6]

. . . I am in
So far in blood that sin will pluck on sin.

[*Richard*—IV. ii. 68–9]

Harp not on that string. . . .

[*Richard*—IV. iv. 409]

O coward conscience, how dost thou afflict me!

[*Richard*—V. iii. 206]

A horse! a horse! my kingdom for a horse!

[*Richard*—V. iv. 7]

. . . I have set my life upon a cast,
And I will stand the hazard of the die.

[*Richard*—V. iv. 9–10]